Teen Pregnancy

ACKNOWLEDGMENTS

*Gloria Parmerlec-Greiner and the
Boulder Valley School Teen-Parenting Class
and all the babies who
contributed to this book.*

*Illustrations and hand lettering
by Linda Gerrard Ely*

Teen Pregnancy
The Challenges We Faced
The Choices We Made

Donna & Rodger Ewy

PRUETT PUBLISHING COMPANY
Boulder, Colorado

©1984 By Donna & Rodger Ewy
All rights reserved, including those to reproduce this book, or parts thereof, in any form, without permission in writing from the Publisher.

First Edition
2 3 4 5 6 7 8 9

Printed in the United States of America

Library of Congress Cataloging in Publication Data
Ewy, Donna.
  Teen pregnancy.

  Summary: A guide for teenagers facing pregnancy including information on nutrition, exercise, childbirth, infant care, and birth control. Also includes first person narratives about what it means to be a teenage parent.
  1. Pregnancy, Adolescent. 2. Childbirth. 3. Infants (Newborn)—Care and hygiene. [1. Pregnancy. 2. Childbirth. 3. Babies—Care and hygiene] I. Ewy, Rodger. II. Title.
RG556.5.E95   1983   618.2'088055   83-17809
ISBN 0-87108-652-2 (pbk.)

CONTENTS

1. The Challenges We Met; The Choices We Made   1
2. Your Baby's Story From Conception To Birth   23
3. Mom's Story Through Nine Months Of Pregnancy   35
4. Advice From Amy   43
5. What Did You Do For Your Baby Today   57
6. Prenatal Care For You and Your Baby   73
7. From Laughter To Tears: Emotional and Social Changes   85
8. How Can I Be Pregnant and Stay In School   107
9. Childbirth: The Greatest Challenge   119
10. Who Is Going To Parent Your Baby   141
11. Parenting: What Do You Do With A Newborn   153
12. Pregnancy: You Do Have A Choice   165

The Challenges We Faced and The Choices We Made

We are writing this book because we think teens will listen to people who have experienced pregnancy and parenthood themselves.

Maria: *I wish that someone had told me ahead of time that sex is not just a game. I know I want my baby, but I am still in school and now I have to work everything out instead of having it easy and enjoying myself like I should be doing. I think I would have been more prepared if someone my own age had put it right in front of me and said, "Look, this is the way it is when you are young and you are pregnant."*

Angela: *I think that both girls and boys should hear us. They should know that it's not fun and games—this is for real. They should understand how important it is to know if you want a baby and how important it is to plan for one.*

Christina: *I think that every guy should think that when he gets a girl pregnant, he is pregnant too. You've both got to think about that baby. A boy should understand that even if he can get a girl pregnant and run away, he is still leaving some little tiny person whose life is still ahead.*

He won't know if his child is going to live in poverty or in a broken home. There is always something missing, even if the mom gives lots and lots of love. There is always a little bit missing without a father.

Stephanie: *We should let every man know exactly what he is leaving behind and what he is putting his child through by not being a father. A father is important. You can give a child all that love and he still will one day ask, "Where is my dad? How come I don't have one? Everybody else does."*

Nancy: *It would be good for teenagers to have us young pregnant teenagers and young parents tell our story. You can see a movie and you can see pictures but it's not the same as real life. Hearing from real live girls with their babies pulling on their hair makes it real, not games.*

CHALLENGES

When you are pregnant and when you are a teen you have special challenges. First, everyone has told us that pregnant teens have a much higher risk during pregnancy. Most of us had something happen. Ten out of twenty-five of us ended up with cesareans during childbirth. Most of us had some kind of anemia during pregnancy and had to really watch our diets. We were all tired. We not only had pregnancy to deal with, but school and some of us had marriage (with housekeeping, cooking, shopping and caring for a husband).

We also had many concerns about how our parents were going to react to the news of our pregnancies. How were the fathers of our babies going to take the news of their fatherhood? How were our friends going to act towards us? What was pregnancy going to do to our schooling? How would it affect our job and career plans? What would pregnancy mean to our personal development and freedom? What kind of parents would we be?

We all had concerns about finances. How were we going to pay for the birth? For those of us who were going to keep our babies, how were we going to afford to buy our babies the things that they needed? How could we support ourselves?

All of us experienced being pregnant while at the same time being teens. None of us were prepared for the special challenges and choices that came with pregnancy. All the books we had read told us that pregnancy was a breeze. They said things like, "During the next nine months you will be your healthiest and with just a little care you can be prettier than you have ever been despite your changing figure. Your skin will be clear and radiant. Your eyes will sparkle with excitement and anticipation."

What we really needed was a book that told us about the first months of pregnancy, what happens in a prenatal exam, how to continue in school, how to get jobs to support ourselves and our babies, what choices of parenting we had, how to get economic assistance, how to parent, and where to get information.

We all agreed we needed information—not assurance that we would look prettier. That's when we decided to develop some of our material. We thought that if we could get to other teens, share our experiences with them, that they would listen to us.

These are the things we would like to share with you: The challenges we faced and the choices we made as we experienced pregnancy, childbirth and parenting.

OUR STORIES:

FROM CHILDHOOD TO MOTHERHOOD

Our ages range from twelve to nineteen. We are all from different backgrounds. All of us had different dreams and hopes for the future. Out of 25 of us, only one of us planned her pregnancy—and she was married. The rest of us—well, we just got pregnant.

Some of us had been sexually active for years and some of us got pregnant the first time we had sex. Some of us were on contraceptives, some of us weren't. Some of us had boyfriends who said they would stick with us. A few of us married after we found out we were pregnant. Some of us hardly even knew the fathers of our babies.

Some of us had parents who gave us support throughout our pregnancies and births. Others of us were kicked out of the house and had to make it on our own.

Some of us chose to marry and keep our babies. Others chose to be single parents, and a few decided to give their babies up for adoption.

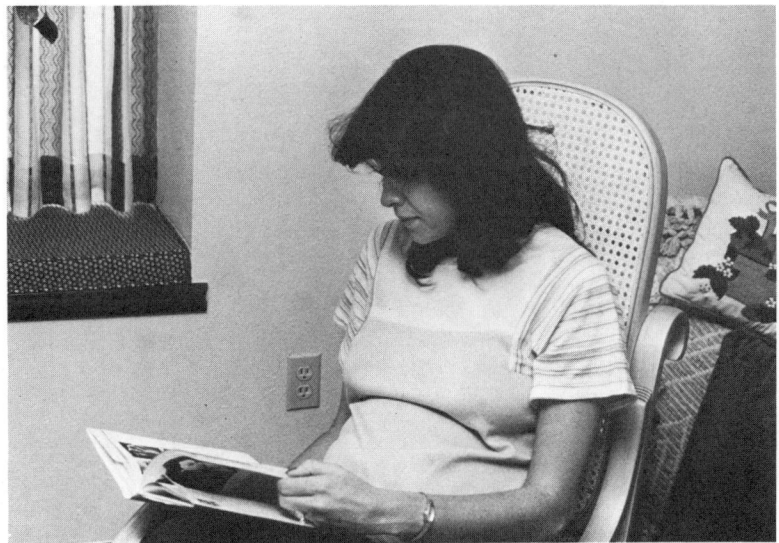

Angela: (16) unmarried

I was really surprised when I got pregnant. Robert and I had been going together and having sex for three years before I got pregnant. I thought that I was either lucky or sterile but I found out different.

Robert accused me of planning the whole thing out. He said that I had sex with him with the intention to get pregnant. He didn't realize how stupid that sounds. "Oh, yes, I wanted to give up my life for you, just so I could trap you."

Robert joined the Navy and I didn't think I would ever see him again. But I decided he wasn't going to get off scott free so I contacted the Navy and he sends me money every month. I'm hurt he doesn't even want to see his own baby.

I want Melissa to know that I wanted things to work out with her father, and I wanted a family, and I wanted her to be happy with her mother and father. But her father wasn't willing to take on that responsibility.

I'm still very young, and I feel like I am a baby. And here I've had a baby.

Kimberly: (17) married

I'd been going with Mark since we were 13. I got pregnant when I was 14, but he made me have an abortion because he told me there was no way that I could be a mother to a kid.

When I was 16 I got pregnant and we decided to get married. It's not been easy though. But, I'm working to make a happy family. We bought a trailer and I try to keep it up. Mark is the kind of guy who works a lot and supports us really well. Sometimes, though, when we fight, it's really hard on the baby.

Sometimes I really miss being in school and having no responsibilities. I watch all my friends go to dances and I have to go home and take care of Bo. Sometimes when we fight, Mark doesn't come home. Other times I go out with my girlfriends and I don't come home. But, we both try and I hope for my baby's sake that we are going to make a go of it.

Holly: (16) unmarried

I ran around with a wild group of kids. We were always at bars or racing around in our jeeps. I came from a small town and couldn't wait to get away from my parents who were always holding me down. I had sex with a lot of guys before Craig but I had been going with him for around a year before I got pregnant. At the time we had plans to be married but three weeks before the marriage he got real cold feet and called it off. When that happened, I was thinking, "Should I give the baby up for adoption or can I handle it? Can I be enough of a parent for both of us?" I've decided to keep my baby. Although my father doesn't want anything to do with me, my mom said she will help me.

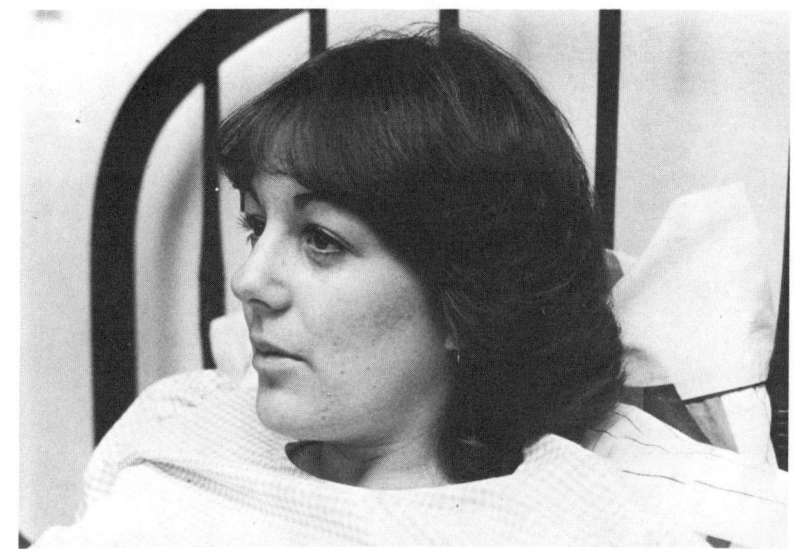

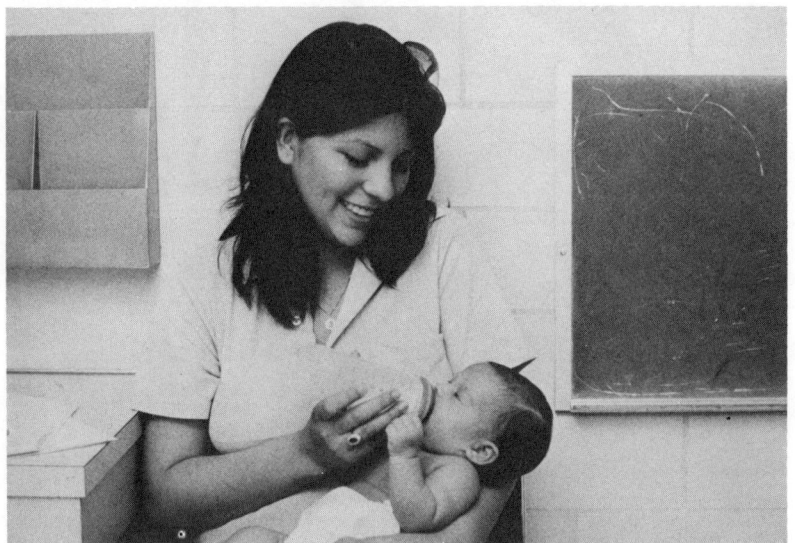

Cheryl: (14) unmarried

Last year, when I was thirteen, I got a job at a drive-in. I started going with the guy who managed it. He talked me into buying a car together. I put in $1600 (all the wages I had earned with him) and he put in $200. When I got pregnant he left town. I found out that he was married and had two other kids to support. He came back and told me he would pay for an abortion but he already owed me $1600 and I didn't think he would. Then he said he was going to sell the car for $6000 and send me the money. I'll believe it when I see it.

I'm going to stay home. My mom is paying for everything. She is even going to childbirth classes with me. My sister worries me. She's kind of jealous over my pregnancy and I'm worried she'll be jealous over the baby. I hope she moves out because I don't want my kid to be like her.

Rachel: (15) unmarried

I never dated much—nobody ever asked me out and I didn't think anyone ever would. All we did was fight at home. My parents never talk with me and I don't want to talk with them. School wasn't much better and I didn't have many friends. When Santos came along he made me feel that I really was somebody. He was from Mexico and didn't know anyone and asked me out. When I got pregnant he disappeared. I called his family in Mexico but they wouldn't let me speak to him.

My father was furious because I had three other sisters who got pregnant when they were teenagers. He was going to kick me out but he didn't.

When I had my baby I had to have a cesarean and I don't have any insurance and am under 16. The hospital sued my parents. I told them I would pay them back but I don't know how I'm going to do it. I'm not sorry for anything. I love my baby. For the first time in my life I feel that I have someone who loves me.

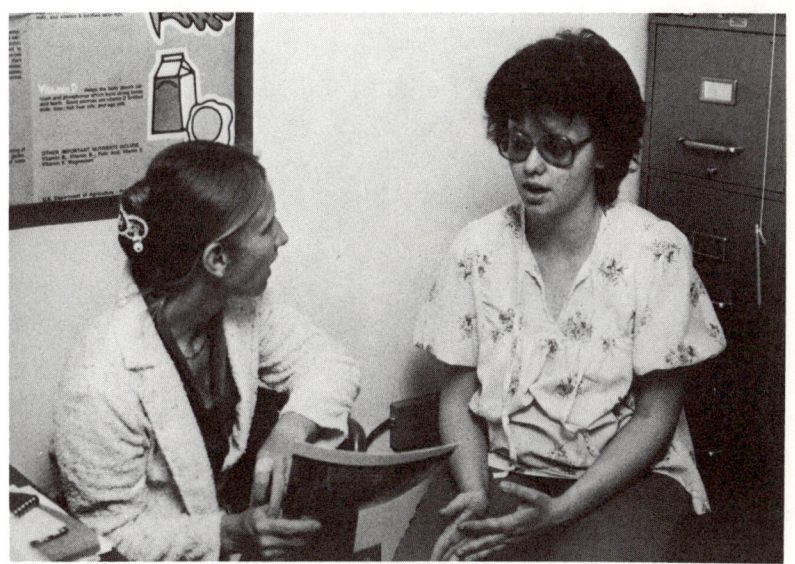

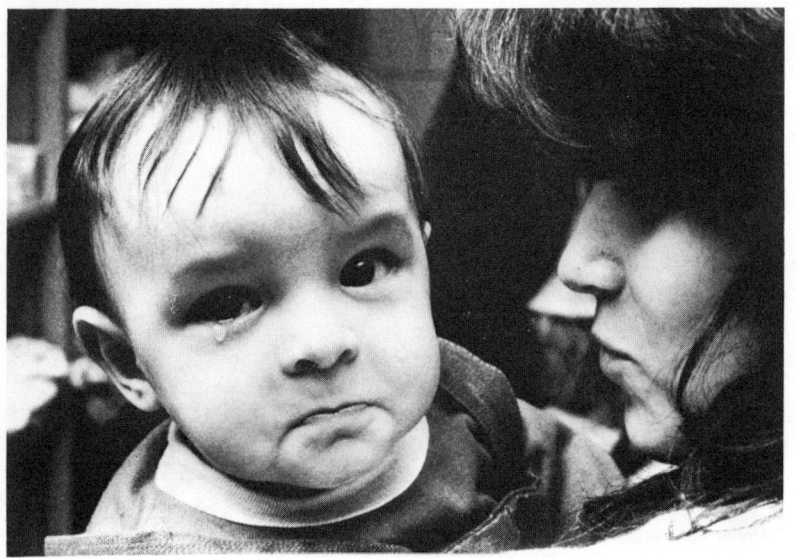

Theresa: (16) married (two babies)

Well, I had a lot of dreams for my life. My mom had died when I was a little girl, my dad left me and I was raised by an aunt. I met my husband in school when I was fourteen. I had planned on going to college after high school. I wanted to get into psychology because I enjoy helping other people, listening to their problems and giving them advice.

When I found I was pregnant I told Paul and he wanted to get married right away. He quit school to get a job to support us and we lived with my aunt.

We had another baby nine months after Sammy was born and Paul was laid off his job just before his birth. I had to drop out of school and try to find a job. Paul feels like he's unwanted and he's jealous of the baby. I love my babies but nothing turned out like I thought it would.

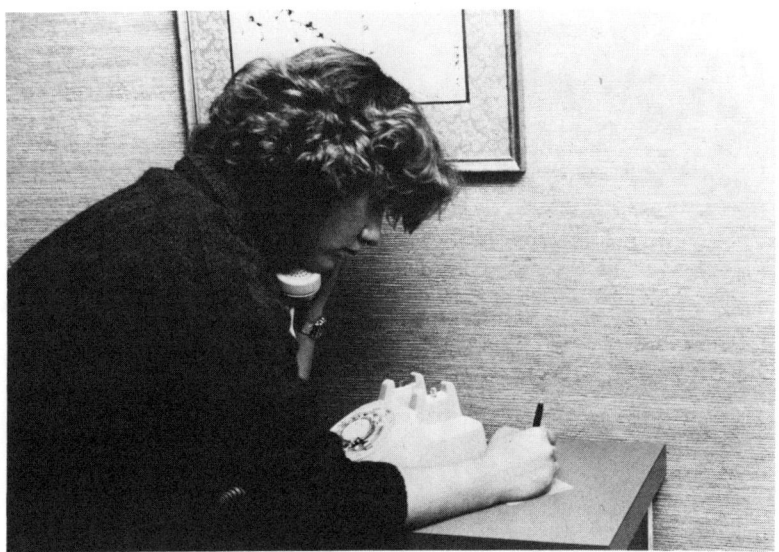

Tammy: (16) unmarried

Ricky and I had been going together for a while before I got pregnant. My mom won't accept it. She blames herself. I keep telling her, "If you would have forbidden me to see him, I would have wanted to see him that much more. Just accept it. What's done is done." She won't. I can't talk to her at all.

When I told Ricky, he was happy at first, but then he dropped out of school and went to another town with his father. He told me he would be back but I don't believe it. Besides, I'm not so sure I want to see him again.

I want to keep my baby but my mom says she doesn't have enough money for my sister and me let alone another baby. I sure can't expect any money from Ricky. I don't know what I'm going to do. I guess having a baby is going to change my life a lot. I had an abortion when I was 13 and don't want to do it again.

Molly: (18) married

My mom and dad got divorced and I hated it. I think that's one of the worst things that ever happened to me, and that's one of the reasons I got pregnant. After my parents got a divorce I ran wild. Because my mom wanted to start dating again and my dad was out somewhere I did whatever I wanted.

I think I wanted to get pregnant because I needed something that was mine. I felt like I had lost something and I wanted something back that I couldn't lose. Michael and I are married now and he has a good job. My parents love the baby. With the teen parent program here I am going to graduate in June. So things are going pretty well.

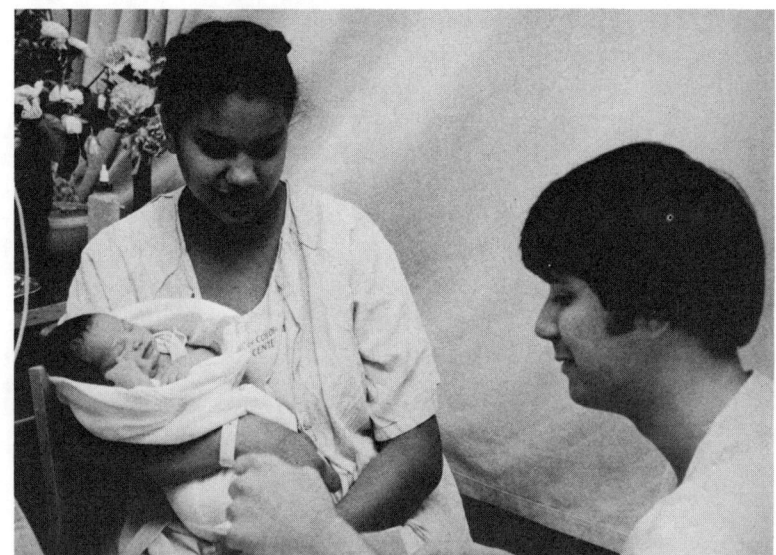

Susie: (13) unmarried

I come from a family where school doesn't make much difference. We never had enough money for a good life anyway and I don't think much about my future. I've known George since we were kids and we were always messing around anyway. When I got pregnant, he asked me, "Who is the father?" He knew that he was the only boy I had ever had sex with. I couldn't believe it. That really hurt me.

I have three other sisters who live at home and have babies and I guess that's what I'll do. I never liked school much anyway.

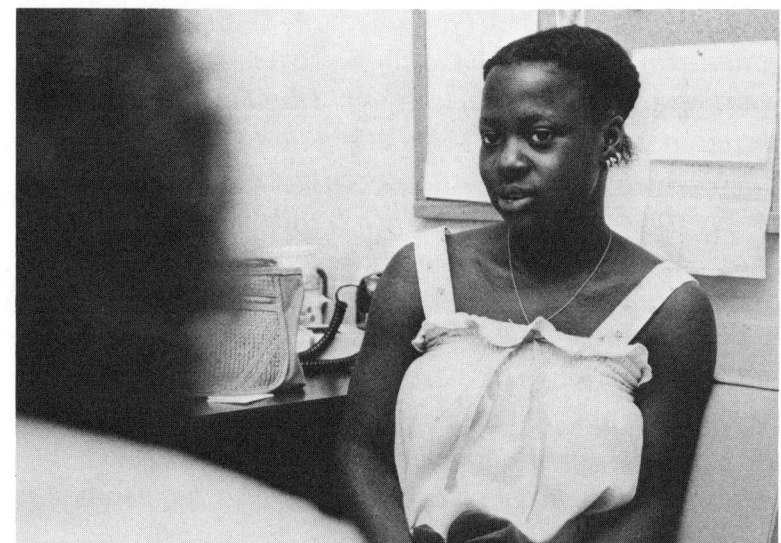

Tina: (18) married

We were married when I was fifteen. My parents had just gotten a divorce and I was drifting all over and I ran off with Steven just to get back at them. I thought that that would make them pay some attention to me.

It was really great because Steven was older. He was twenty-three and he had a good job and could take care of me. When I got pregnant three months later he was really happy. He's a good father and really loves our baby.

Sometimes, when I look at my other friends, I wish that I were single and free again. But I've got a husband who loves me and a great daughter. I'm going to school and learning how to do data processing. I'm also doing some modeling on the side so I guess my life is pretty good.

I don't want to have another kid for a long time because this twenty-four-hour-a-day responsibility is really hard. Steven doesn't like it either, but we are trying to make a good marriage. I am lucky to have him.

Maria: (16) unmarried

Thomas and I have been going together since I was fourteen. We knew that we wanted to get married, but Thomas had big plans. He was going to get a scholarship to a college and we were going to get married later.

We never had sex—only once—and that's all it took. I got pregnant the first time and I didn't even enjoy it.

Thomas was very excited at first. He told me he would support me and that we could get married. But I didn't want to marry him like that and have him hold it against me for the rest of my life. Every time he looked at our baby he would think that she caused him to give everything up. Well, as the months went by, Thomas got less and less interested and excited. Finally, he was hardly coming by.

When the baby was born he came to visit her in the hospital, and he comes by every once in a while but he doesn't act like a daddy and I resent it. He still wants to go to college and get married when he gets out but I'm not going to wait four years. I've got my own life. Although my parents have been great, they think my baby is theirs. I've got to get out somehow. I'm really disappointed with how everything has turned out. I love my baby but I'll always wonder when Deja says, "Why didn't you marry my daddy?" I'm going to think, "Did I do the right thing? Did I make a big mistake in not waiting?"

Christina: (17) unmarried

I come from a family where you just don't get pregnant. But all my friends were into sex and here I was 17. I thought I should be into it too. I didn't believe you could get pregnant the first time but I did. Just my luck. When I told my boyfriend he left me. He said he didn't want a baby and that this baby wasn't his. I was really hurt because he told me before that he wanted me to have his baby. That's why I had sex with him. My parents were furious and I had to leave my town. I hitchhiked out to Colorado and I'm staying with a friend now.

I know I can't keep my baby. I can't give it all the things a baby needs and I sure can't dump it on my parents because they can't afford to take care of their own family.

I've decided to give it up for adoption. I think it's better for the baby to give it to parents who can't have a baby themselves. I think that I'm really doing a favor to my baby although I'm always going to wonder what it looks like and what it's doing.

Rebecca: (15) unmarried

I thought, "It can't be me. It can't be happening to me." I felt guilty. I came home and told my mom right away. I hated to tell my parents. The father of my baby was nice to me until he found out I was pregnant. And now he doesn't want to have anything to do with me. He's going around telling everybody he doesn't even know me. That really hurts.

When I was little, I always thought that when I got older I would get married, and have kids, and just be a housewife. I didn't feel like I wanted to travel or see the world. I have always wanted to be a homemaker and a mother. Now I know I made a mistake because I picked the wrong guy.

My Dad has been supporting me. And my grandmother says, "Everyone makes mistakes—it's only human."

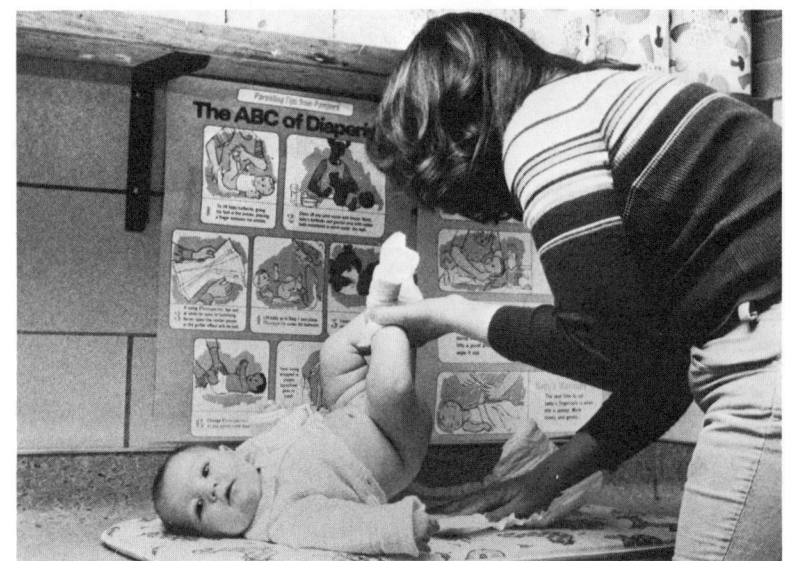

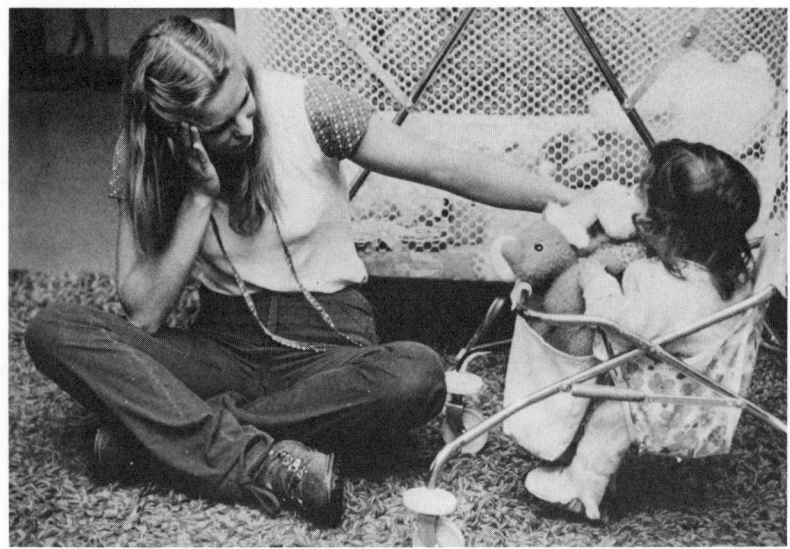

Nancy: (19) divorced

When I found out I was pregnant I felt guilty. How was I going to break it to my parents? They took it pretty bad when they first found out. My boyfriend agreed to marry me. After we were married we had a pretty hard time. We fought a lot. He didn't want to stay home and he didn't have the maturity to be a husband let alone a father. When he left me he said that he would send child support. He did for a few months, but I haven't heard from him since.

Money, money, money is my biggest problem now. I don't even have a high school diploma and it's so hard to find a decent job and pay for my babysitting on top of it. I have rent, food, clothing and nothing left over to buy Crystal the things I would like to.

I'd like to date, but I'm so tired when I come home. And, besides, I can't quite trust guys now. When they ask me out they think, "Divorced lady, easy city." It's just not worth the hassle. Besides, it's pretty hard to find someone who will accept both me and Crystal.

Robyn: (18) unmarried

I dated John for about a year. He always told me that if anything ever happened he would take care of me. When I told him I was pregnant he said that it wasn't his baby. He dropped me and started dating my best friend.

It was hard for me to accept that he didn't care as much as he said he did before I got pregnant. And it was kind of a shock.

I was so mad and hurt. But then I decided, "Who needs him?" My parents hired a lawyer and now he has to pay some of his wages each month to support his baby.

I figure I got off easy—who wants some creep like that? It's going to be John who suffers because he isn't going to be there to see the first smile and the first step. He's going to miss all that.

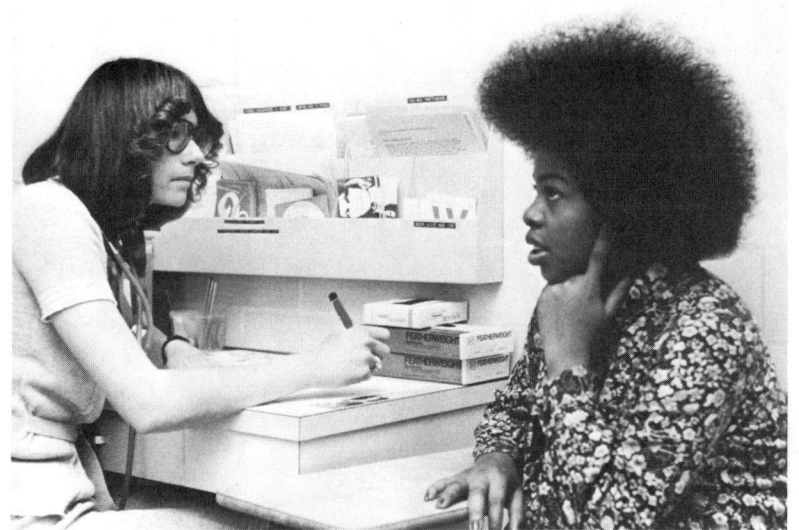

CHOICES

Well, teen pregnancy may be full of challenges but it doesn't mean that all is lost. You can have a healthy baby and a happy life. You just have to make some very special choices. These are the choices we found made the difference.

FIRST: You have to get early prenatal care so both you and your baby can have a healthy experience.

SECOND: You, and only you, can get the food both you and your baby need for good nutrition.

THIRD: You, and only you, can continue to get the education that will affect you and your baby for the rest of your life.

FOURTH: You can choose to take advantage of vocational and job training programs.

FIFTH: It is important that you develop a support system of people you can rely on for emotional, physical, financial and even spiritual support—you and your baby are going to need it.

SIXTH: Choose to go to childbirth classes that will prepare you to be an active participant in the birth of your baby.

SEVENTH: Whether you are married or not, it's important that you get information about marriage: what it is and how to make the most of it.

EIGHTH: Get information about the pros and cons before you make a decision whether to keep or relinquish your baby.

NINTH: And, finally, it's important you get information about sexuality and contraceptives.

That's what this book is all about. What the choices are, and how to make them.

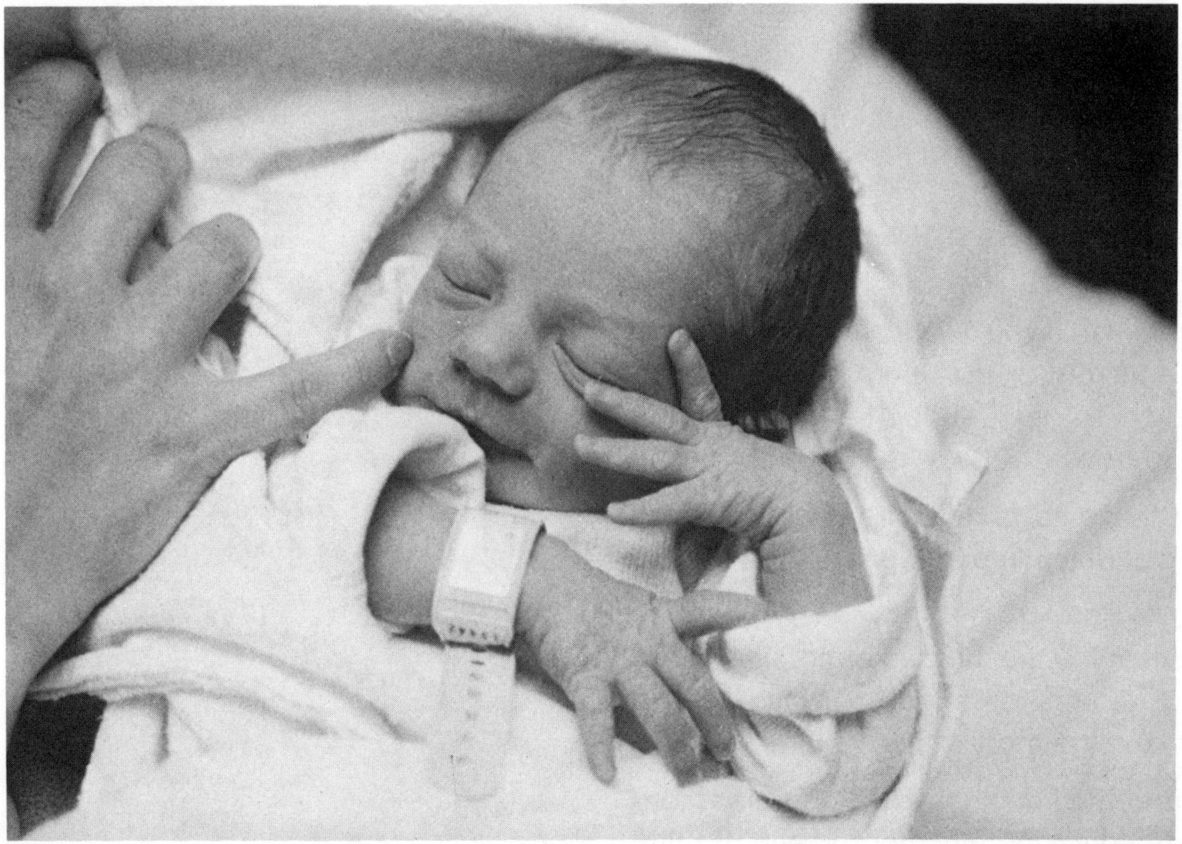

Your Baby's Story From Conception to Birth

CHALLENGE:

Even before you suspect that you are pregnant your baby is developing with amazing speed. Although he may be only a quarter of an inch long, his spine, brain and heart are already advanced in development.

CHOICE:

How you choose to care for yourself in these early days is vital to your baby's healthy start in life.

QUOTE:

"I think it's a miracle to feel your baby in you, to feel it kicking and turning and to know that it's your baby. It makes you really wonder. You know that the baby is completely dependent on you for everything—for it's life!"

QUESTIONS:

What is an egg and where does it come from?
What does the uterus do?
Why do you menstruate?
When is the time a woman can get pregnant?
What are sperm? Where do they come from?
How do sperm get to the egg?
What will my baby look like?
What determines whether a baby is a girl or a boy?
How do you get twins?
Where does the baby get its food and air?
When do you begin to feel the baby kick?
When can you hear the baby's heartbeat?
When do you begin to wear maternity clothes?
How early can a baby be born and live on its own?
How big is a newborn baby?
What is the "bag of waters"?
What is the "afterbirth"?
Can a baby see in the uterus?
What does my baby hear in the uterus?

CONCEPTION

An egg by itself cannot become a child.
A sperm by itself cannot become a child.
One egg + one sperm = one child.

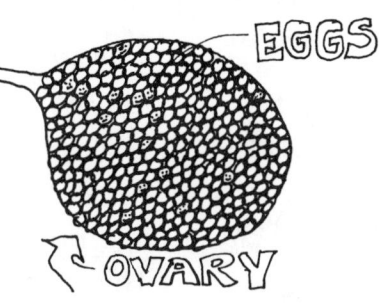

The way that the egg and sperm get together is through intercourse (making love or having sexual relations). You yourself are a product of your mother's egg and your father's sperm and the way that you got here was through sexual intercourse. And, when you have a baby, your child will be a combination of an egg and a sperm brought together through intercourse. That's the way things have been and it looks like that's the way things are going to be.

WHERE DO EGGS COME FROM?

You, the mom, are born with about 250,000 eggs. There are two sacs, called ovaries, that carry all these eggs. These eggs are usually in an immature state, but once every month an egg from one of the ovaries matures, ripens, moves to the surface on the ovary and pops out into your abdominal cavity. This moment is called *ovulation*. The egg then swims around looking for a sperm. At the same time the fallopian tube, a tube attached to your uterus, acts like a suction tube and draws the egg into your uterus.

WHAT DOES THE UTERUS DO?

If the egg has been fertilized with a sperm, the uterus will become a home where the embryo will find all the shelter, food, comfort and warmth that it needs to survive. Your uterus is about the size and shape of a pear. To imagine what your uterus looks like, place your fist against your stomach right above your pubic bone. That's just about the right size and position. The top of your hand would be about where the fallopian tubes come out. The middle of your fist is about where the ovaries are attached. The uterus is made out of muscle tissue and is designed to grow and stretch over fifty times its original size during pregnancy.

Your uterus resembles a balloon turned upside down. At the bottom, there is an opening just like the opening of a balloon. This opening, called the cervix (or neck) of the uterus, is a thick muscular band designed to help the sperm enter. It closes up when the egg becomes fertilized.

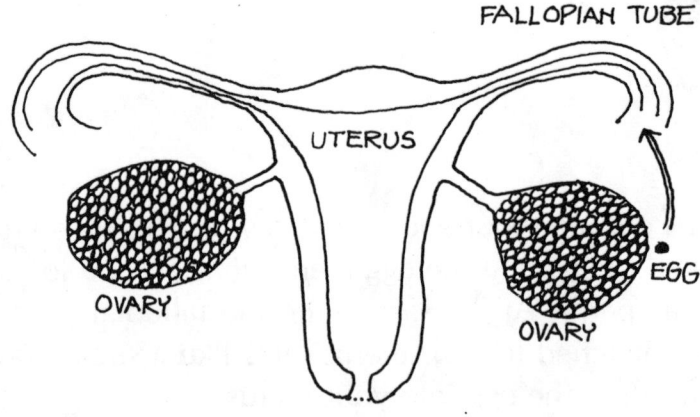

THEN WHAT IS MENSTRUATION?

If the egg is not fertilized (that is, no sperm are present), the egg simply passes through your uterus out your vagina and the lining of the uterus is shed during what we call *menstruation*.

WHEN IS THE TIME A WOMAN CAN GET PREGNANT MOST EASILY?

Most women experience a monthly cycle that is geared to receiving a fertilized egg. All of this is going on in your body and you are barely even aware of it.

Days 1-5: Menstruation is the most evident (and least important) part of your cycle as your uterine lining is being shed. This is often called a "period." The period comes every 28-32 days. Most women have a total flow of about eight tablespoons of blood and tissue shed over a 3-5 day period.

Days 6-13: These are the days that your uterus is building up the rich lining to receive a fertilized egg.

Day 14: Ovulation is the most important part of your cycle. It is the day (in a twenty-eight day cycle) that the egg bursts forth and is swept into the fallopian tube. This is the time when you are most fertile and the time that you will most likely get pregnant.

Days 15-21: The uterus (still hoping that the egg has been fertilized) keeps building up a lining.

Days 22-28: During these days, the egg, if fertilized, will attach and nestle into the lining of the uterus. If the egg is not fertilized, it withers and passes out of your body and the uterus prepares to shed the lining.

Days 1-5: Menstruation and the cycle begin anew.

OTHER OVULATION CYCLES: During your teen years it is not unusual to experience irregular cycles from 25-50 days. If your cycle is irregular, the day of ovulation (and your fertile period) will vary greatly. Ovulation does NOT come halfway between cycles but usually *14 days BEFORE the next cycle*. So if you experience a 25 day cycle, you probably will ovulate on day 11. If you experience a 70 day cycle, ovulation can occur on day 56. If you are irregular, it's next to impossible to know when it is 14 days before your next period because you don't know when your next period will come.

HOW DOES AN EGG GET FERTILIZED?

An egg can be fertilized only during that part of your cycle when the egg has ripened, has been released and is in the upper part of your fallopian tube. Nature does everything it can do to ensure conception: The egg can survive for up to two days, during which time it can be fertilized. Sperm cells can stay alive for two to three days. Some say the sperm can live for up to ten days! If you have had intercourse up to ten days before ovulation, the sperm can be there waiting to fertilize the egg. Or if you have intercourse a couple of days after ovulation, the egg can be fertilized. Although you ovulate on only one day, the egg could be fertilized over a period of 12 days.

Nature has one thing in mind for the egg: fertilization. Nature wants you pregnant and does everything she can do during your fertile period to get you pregnant. In fact, if teen girls use no protection, they can count on getting pregnant within 18 months of becoming sexually active. 20 out of 100 pregnant teens get pregnant the FIRST time they have intercourse.

WHERE DO SPERM COME FROM?

You, the dad, provide the sperm. These sperm have only one mission in life: to fertilize an egg and make you a father! Millions of sperm are released during intercourse and they engage in a great race to get to the egg.

Two organs about the size and shape of ping-pong balls hang on either side of the penis. These organs are called testes. The sperm mature and ripen inside the testes. When they are mature they are released into organs in your body where they combine with nutrients and fluids to make semen.

The penis has a tube called a urethra that is designed to allow urine to pass through the penis in its relaxed state. But, when the penis becomes erect, the bladder is closed off, a cleansing agent is sent through the urethra, and only the semen is allowed to pass through.

HOW DOES THE SPERM GET TO THE EGG?

Special things happen when a man and woman become sexually excited. The brain sends the message to all of your body, but especially to your genitals. The penis becomes bigger and stiffer and prepared for action. The sperm, which have been waiting for the moment, are ready to escape through the opening of the penis. When the penis is in the vagina and the man comes (climaxes or has an orgasm), the sperm are shot out in a small forceful stream. This is called an ejaculation. The strong contractions drive the semen out the end of the penis into the vagina. Each ejaculation contains from two to five million sperm so you can see nature isn't fooling around. In fact, the sperm are so intent on getting to the egg that even if the penis is not in the vagina (such as if the man withdraws his penis to prevent pregnancy) sperm can sometimes swim into the vagina from the outside.

JOURNEY OF THE SPERM TO THE EGG

Once in the vagina, the race is on! Lashing their tails back and forth, the sperm sweep their way through the cervix and uterus and swim into the tube where the egg is irresistably attractive. Sperm are so intent to get to the egg that they are known to swim around diaphragms, through leaky condoms, through spermicidal jellies and against all odds to fertilize the egg. Sperm, swimming at the rate of one inch in eight minutes, reach the impatiently waiting egg in an hour to an hour and a half. The strongest and the fastest sperm is the first to reach the egg. Dropping off its tail, the sperm digs into the egg, triggering a chemical change that turns away all other sperm.

WHAT WILL YOUR BABY LOOK LIKE?

The mother's egg carries 23 chromosomes. These chromosomes carry all the information about eye color, hair color, skin color and even the basis for personality and behavior that comes from your side of the family. The father's sperm also carries 23 chromosomes. When the egg and sperm fertilize, the real contest is on.

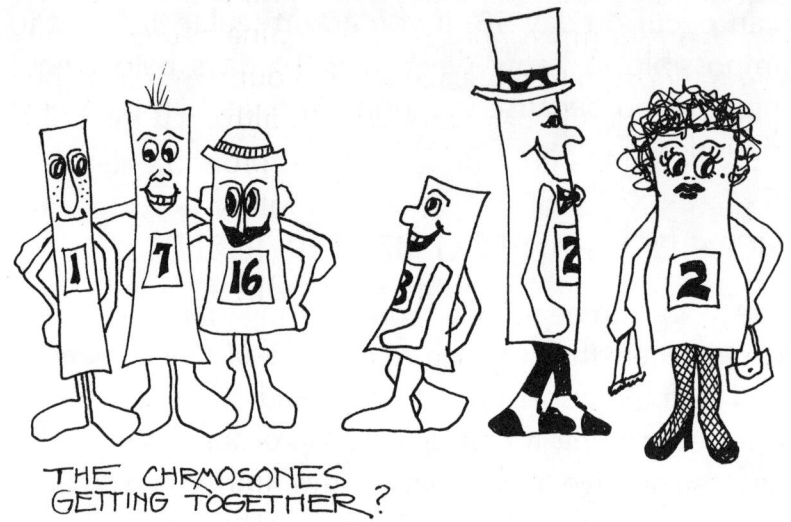

THE CHRMOSONES GETTING TOGETHER?

The chromosomes carry genes that determine the baby's characteristics. The genes can be dominant or recessive. Dominant means that that particular characteristic will show up in the baby, and recessive means that it will not show up in the baby but the baby will carry the genes to pass on to his/her own child. Now, if the mom's gene is blue eyes and the dad's gene is brown eyes, what color will the baby's be? If the dominant gene is brown, and the recessive gene for eyes is blue, you can expect the baby to have brown eyes. If, however, the dad's mother had blue eyes (and although he has brown eyes he still carries a blue-eyed gene), there is a chance that the baby might have blue eyes or perhaps green, grey or hazel eyes from a mixture of the two genes.

It's fun to think about what your baby will look like. Because we know that black hair is dominant over blonde, dark skin dominant over light, tallness dominant over shortness, big noses dominant over small, you may begin to fantasize about your own baby. But remember that genes can mix and although the baby may resemble either of you, it will probably turn out to be a mixture of its mother and father.

WHAT SEX WILL YOUR BABY BE?

One of the most fascinating tricks of nature is how the sex of your baby is determined. One of the 23 chromosomes determines the sex of a child. This is called the sex chromosome. The mother carries two sex chromosomes that we call XX. The father carries two similar chromosomes but one of his chromosomes is an X while the other one is a Y. If the father's X chromosome matches up with the mother's X chromosome, the baby will be a girl. If the father's Y chromosome matches up with the mother's X chromosome, the baby will be a boy. So it's really the father's sex chromosome that determines the sex of the baby.

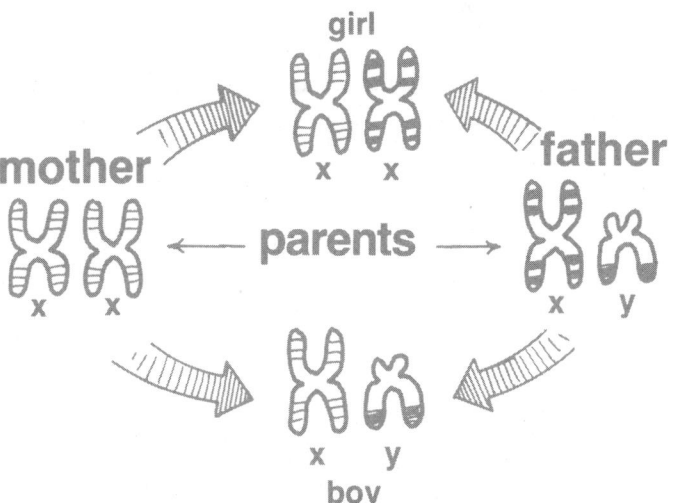

Identical Twins

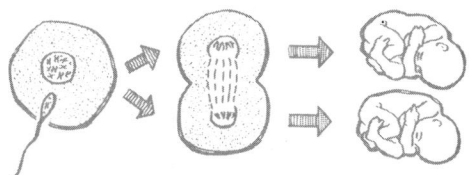

Fraternal Twins

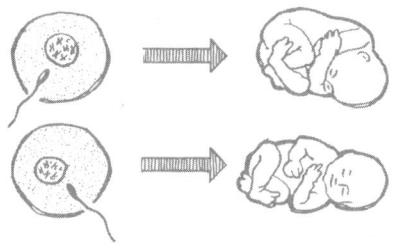

HOW DO YOU GET TWINS?

Although no one knows why, in some cases the fertilized egg immediately divides into two complete but identical twins, each with the same chromosomes. Identical twins are always of the same sex and similar appearance.

Occasionally during a cycle, two eggs are released. If this happens, the two eggs may be fertilized by two different sperm, and "fraternal" twins result. Since fraternal twins result from two sperm and two eggs they are no more alike than any other two children of the same parents.

your baby's development:
FROM A BABY'S EYE VIEW

Hi, Mom, it's my turn now. Come follow me through the nine most important months of my life.

FIRST WEEK: Even during the first week great changes are taking place. It takes me three days to travel down your fallopian tube on my journey to your uterus. On the fourth day I shoot out of the tube and am wandering about your uterus looking for a home. By the sixth day I nestle into the lining of your uterus where it is warm and cozy. And, as my own nourishment from the egg has been all used up, I am relieved to get nourishment from the lining you have prepared for me.

SECOND WEEK: Not only am I growing and changing physically, but I am beginning to develop a sac that will enclose me in a protective fluid until birth. A *placenta* is beginning to develop that will provide the oxygen and nourishment I will get from you. By the end of the second week I resemble a tiny ball.

THIRD WEEK: During my third week an amazing thing happens. The cells arrange themselves into three layers. From these layers come all my body organs. By the fourth week (when I am 1/16 of an inch long), you can see my brain and spine. My heart begins to beat on the twenty-fifth day.

FIRST MONTH: During the first month, when you probably still don't even know you have me, my arms, legs and head form. I can move, open and close my mouth and even swallow. I begin to develop a circulation separate from yours. And now an umbilical cord joins me to the placenta. I am now the size of a pea. I measure ¼ inch long and weigh 1/100 of an ounce.

SECOND MONTH: By the second month my major body organs and systems are developing. My first bone cells have appeared. My eyelids form but their edges are sealed to protect me during my formation. You can see the beginnings of my arms, legs, elbows, knees, fingers, toes, and ears. By the end of the second month I am about the size of a walnut. I am one inch long and weigh about 1/30 of an ounce.

THIRD MONTH: By the third month, you can tell what sex I am and my fingers and toes are distinct and have soft nails. Twenty buds for my baby teeth are present. My brain begins to send signals for movement. By the end of the third month I am about the size of a small lemon. I have increased my length to three inches and I weigh about an ounce.

ONE	TWO	THREE	FOUR	FIVE	SIX
PEA	WALNUT	LEMON	ORANGE	GRAPE-FRUIT	ACORN SQUASH

FOURTH MONTH: Hey, Mom, I'm alive and well and, if you didn't know it before, you are probably becoming quite aware of me now. This may be the time when you feel my first movements. It may feel like the fluttering of butterfly wings but it soon changes to real thumps. I am always looking for the best and most comfortable position. I am now the size of a large orange. I am six to seven inches long and I weigh about four ounces.

FIFTH MONTH: If you haven't gotten into maternity clothes before, you will now. I am growing with astonishing speed and you can see some hair on my head and eyebrows. I'm even getting eyelashes. This may be the first month you can hear my heart and know that I am really in here. By this month I am sleeping and waking at regular intervals. I turn around and around head over heels. By the end of this month I am about the size of a large grapefruit. I weigh about ¾ of a pound.

SIXTH MONTH: By this time you can feel me through your abdomen. Although I now look like a miniature baby, my systems are still immature and I cannot live unaided outside my protective environment. If you could see me during this period of my development you might find my skin quite wrinkled and red and covered by fine soft hair. By the end of this month I am about the size of a large squash. I measure eleven to fourteen inches and weigh about one to one and a half pounds.

SEVENTH MONTH: This is the period of my most rapid growth. I still look quite red and covered with wrinkles. I may suck my thumb and open and close my eyes. I can see light and I can hear your voice. The sound of your heartbeat is my first lesson in rhythm. By the end of the seventh month I am the size of a large cantaloupe. I am about fifteen inches long and weigh almost three pounds.

EIGHTH MONTH: In the eighth month, I grow in size and weight. My wrinkles are being filled out by fat and I'm beginning to look like the baby you have dreamed about. I could probably survive birth if I were born now. I am the size of a small melon. I now measure from sixteen to eighteen inches and weigh about four pounds.

NINTH MONTH: Okay, Mom, get ready for me! My face, head, and body have filled out. I am ready for my journey to the outside world. As you probably have guessed, I am just about the size of a watermelon. By now I weigh a little more than seven pounds and am about twenty inches long.

SEVEN	EIGHT	NINE
CANTALOUPE	SMALL MELON	WATERMELON

MY INNER WORLD

Before I leave you, I would like to share with you a little of my world and the perfect parenting that you have been giving me. Like a spaceman, I have my own space capsule (the amniotic sac), I have my own lifeline (my umbilical cord), and I have my own space pack (the placenta).

AMNIOTIC SAC: My space capsule is the space called the amniotic cavity. This space has a smooth, slippery lining called the *amniotic sac*. My amniotic sac is filled with liquid called *amniotic fluids*. Sometimes mothers call this the "bag of waters." This fluid keeps me warm and protects me from outside injury. The amount of fluid present in this space decreases as I grow larger and larger.

UMBILICAL CORD: My *umbilical cord* is my lifeline. One end of it connects with the placenta, the other leads into my belly at the point that will become my navel after birth. My cord is long and flexible enough to allow me to move freely about. I never breathe air into my lungs until after I am born. Until then, I get oxygen from your blood through the placenta.

PLACENTA: My *placenta* is my space pack. It is pancake shaped and performs as my kidneys, intestines, liver, and lungs. The placenta is also called the "afterbirth" when it is expelled after I am born.

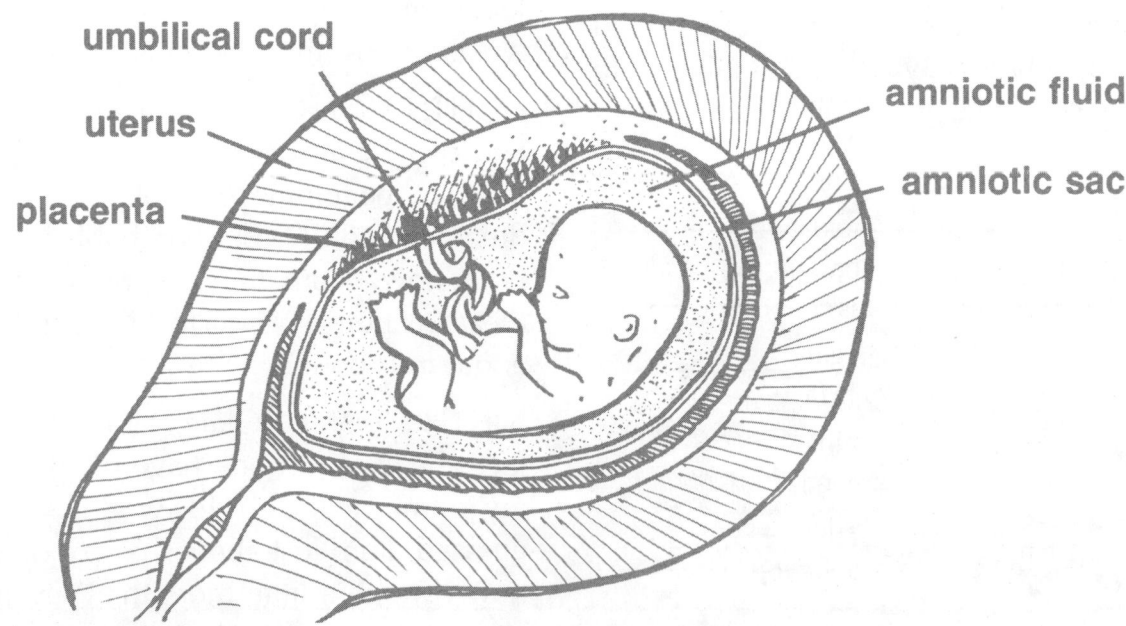

FETAL DEVELOPMENT	FETAL ORGANS	MEASUREMENTS
FIRST MONTH (Embryo)	Brain and beginning of spine evident; vital organs forming.	Length: 1/16" (size increased 10,000 times)
FIFTH WEEK	Heart begins to beat and circulate blood; arm and leg buds emerge; brain, spinal cord, and nervous system established.	Length: 3/16"
SIXTH WEEK	Digestive system forming; arms and legs begin to grow.	Length: 1/4"
SEVENTH WEEK	Umbilical cord joins embryo to placenta; long bones and internal organs developing.	Length: 1/2"; weight: 1/1000 ounce
SECOND MONTH (Fetus)	Human face, arms, legs, fingers, toes, elbows, knees, eyelids, and bone cells forming.	Length: 1"; weight: 1/30 ounce
THIRD MONTH (12 weeks)	Sex distinguishable; fingers and toes moving; teeth buds present; kidney and bladder form.	Length: 3-4"; weight: 1/2-1 ounce
FOURTH MONTH (16 weeks)	Baby moves and kicks, sleeps and wakes, swallows; hair forms, digestion active; pink in color, large head.	Length: 6-7"; weight: 4 ounces
FIFTH MONTH (20 weeks)	Spurt in baby's growth; internal organs maturing; hair, eyebrows, and lashes present; baby increases storage of iron.	Length: 8-12"; weight: 1/2 pound
SIXTH MONTH (24 weeks)	Baby's skin wrinkled, red covered by lanugo and vernix; audible heartbeat.	Length: 11-14"; weight: 1-1 1/2 pounds
SEVENTH MONTH (28 weeks)	Most rapid growth; red and wrinkled; eyelids can open and close; baby storing large amounts of calcium and iron; fetus has chance of surviving if born.	Length: 15"; weight: 3 pounds
EIGHTH MONTH (32 weeks)	Weight gain and rapid growth; settles in favorite position; valuable fat increase.	Length: 16-18"; weight: 4-5 pounds
NINTH MONTH (36 weeks)	Baby gains ½ pound per week; bones of head are soft and flexible; baby has developed immunities.	Length: 18"; weight: 6 pounds
BIRTH (38-42 weeks)	Organs developed; respiratory system mature; mature and firm fingers.	Length: 20"; weight: 7-8 pounds (20 billion cells)

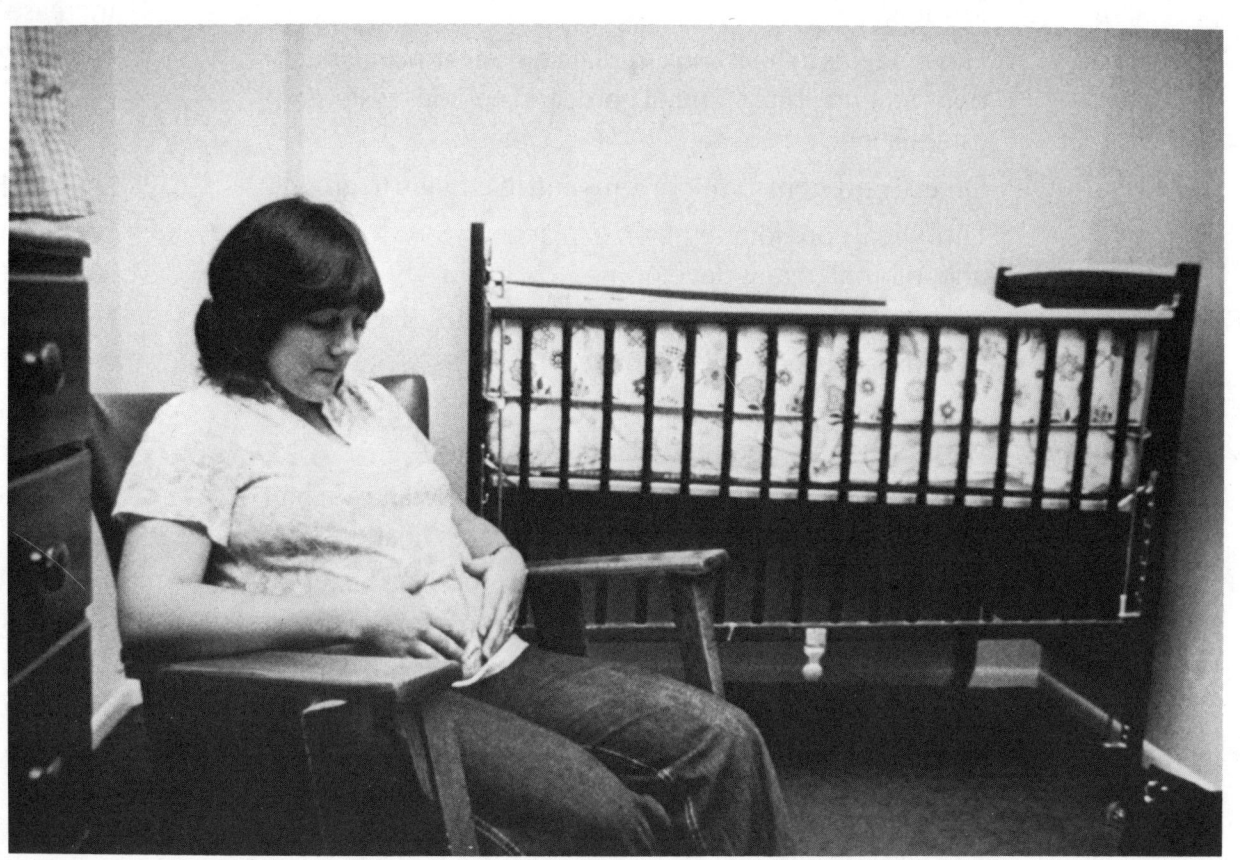

Mom's Story Through Nine Months of Pregnancy

CHALLENGE:

As a pregnant teen, your body not only continues to develop but must also adjust to your baby's growth. Many things are going on to keep your baby healthy and safe in your uterus. Sometimes their side effects may cause you discomfort.

CHOICES:

It's important you know why your body is changing and how, with information and a little effort, you can prevent or lessen many of the common discomforts.

QUOTE:

"My biggest problem is the changes. I can feel myself changing, but I can't explain to myself or to my boyfriend the changes with my body, inside and out. I can't explain why one minute I feel like I'm on top of the world and the next I'm so depressed."

QUESTIONS:

How can you tell you are pregnant?
When do you begin to show?
When can you hear the baby's heartbeat?
What are stretchmarks? Is there anything I can do to prevent stretchmarks?
How do they figure the due date?
What causes morning sickness? Can you have it all day?
Why am I so tired all the time?
I've been constipated all through this pregnancy. Is there anything I can do?
I'm up one minute and down the next. Is this normal?
I can't keep anything down. Is this dangerous for the baby?
My mother got varicose veins. Is there any way I can prevent them?
I have a lot of pain in my back and it seems to be getting worse. Is there anything I can do?
Is there anything I can do to prevent these terrible cramps in my legs?
I'm in my last month of pregnancy and can't seem to get my breath. Is that normal?

MOM'S PHYSICAL CHANGES

YOUR DEVELOPMENT

First Month:

Although you probably don't even feel pregnant the first month, there are great changes taking place within your body. The greatest change takes place within your uterus as it prepares to receive your baby. As your baby implants in the uterus, you first might notice nausea or "morning sickness." You may also notice a swelling and tenderness in your breasts. You may feel more tired than usual. This is the month when you miss your first period.

Second Month:

Increased pressure on your bladder will cause you to want to urinate more frequently. You may experience "all day" sickness because of hormones in your system. Some mothers develop cravings for unusual foods such as pickles and ice cream. Toward the end of this month the placenta and your baby's umbilical cord are starting to develop.

Third Month:

You may notice your abdomen and breasts growing. Fortunately you may feel less "morning sickness" and less bladder pressure. You may notice a thick, yellow substance coming from your nipples. This is colostrum, the first nourishment your baby will get if you decide to breastfeed.

Fourth Month:

Up to now you may have been able to hide your pregnancy. But now there is a great spurt in your baby's growth and your abdomen starts to grow. This is the month when you may feel your baby's first movements and begin to realize that you are really carrying a baby. Increased hormones and your baby's growth may cause you to experience a feeling of fullness, gas or heartburn. You may also notice dark blotches on your face and abdomen.

Fifth Month:

Your uterus expands and your abdomen stretches and your baby's heartbeat can be heard. Your baby's growth may cause pressure against your rectum and cause constipation. Pressure against the blood vessels in your pelvic floor and legs may cause varicose veins or hemorrhoids to occur.

Sixth Month:

This is the time of your greatest weight gain. Your baby is kicking hard and you can feel his arms and legs through your abdomen. The "mask of pregnancy," a darkened area around your eyes, may appear. There also may be a line of heavy pigmentation between

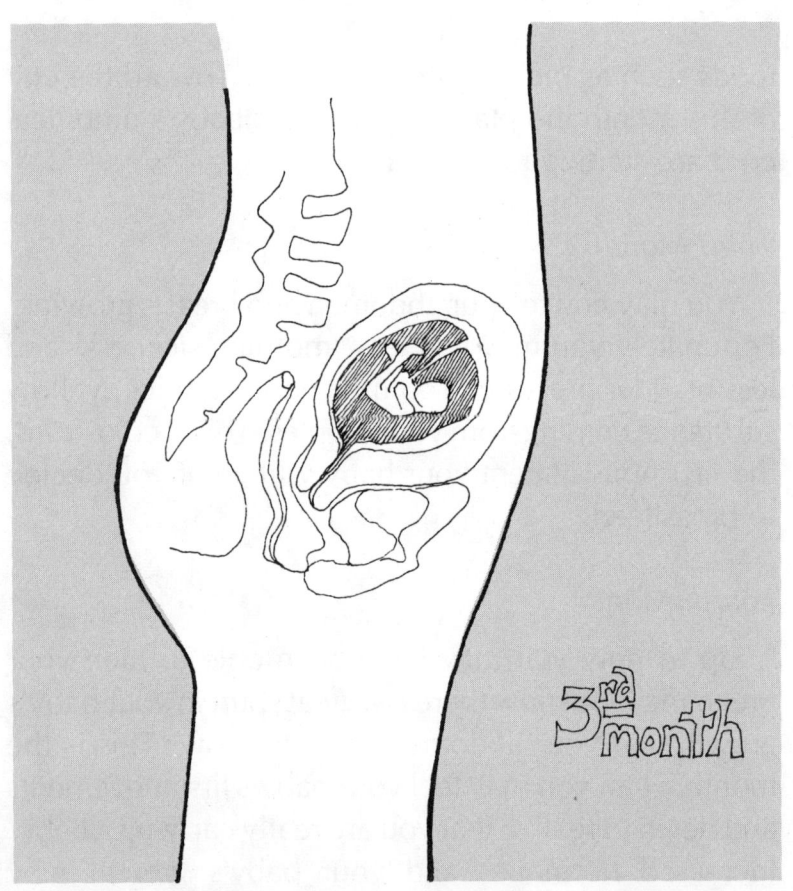

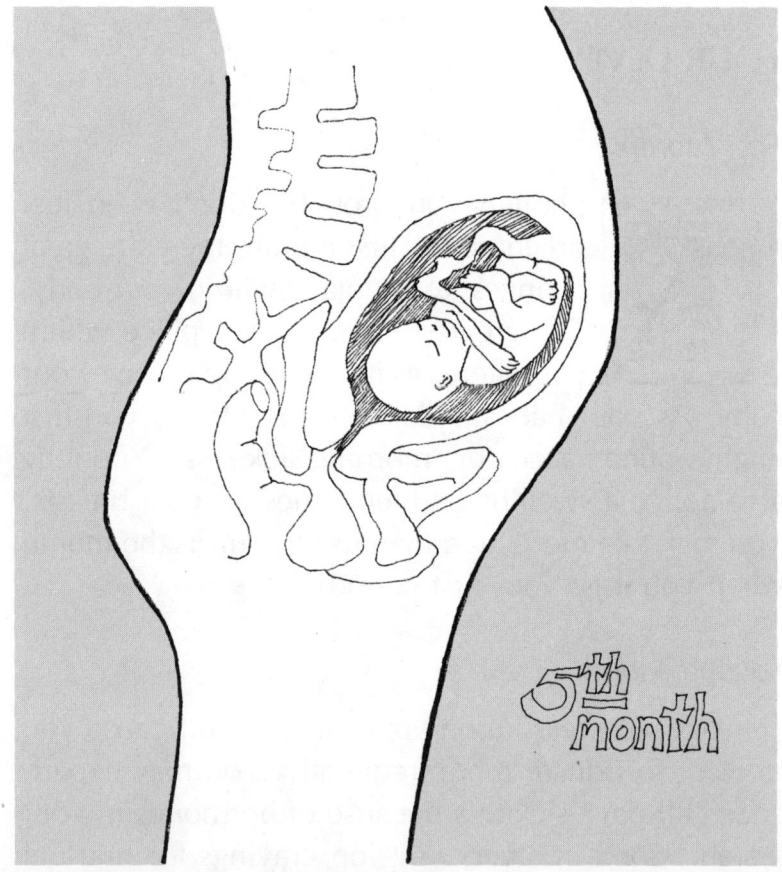

your navel and pubis. Stretching ligaments can cause pains in your groin. Because your baby is increasing his store of iron at this stage, your own iron level begins to drop.

Seventh Month:

Your baby continues to enlarge and his movements become more vigorous. His increased growth puts additional stress on all your systems. Backache is common. You may have nosebleeds. You may notice stretch marks on your abdomen. Your own blood volume increases as your baby's needs increase.

Eighth Month:

This is the month of your baby's most rapid weight gain. His movements are so strong that the arm and leg movements can even be seen from the outside. Because hormones are softening your pelvic joints for

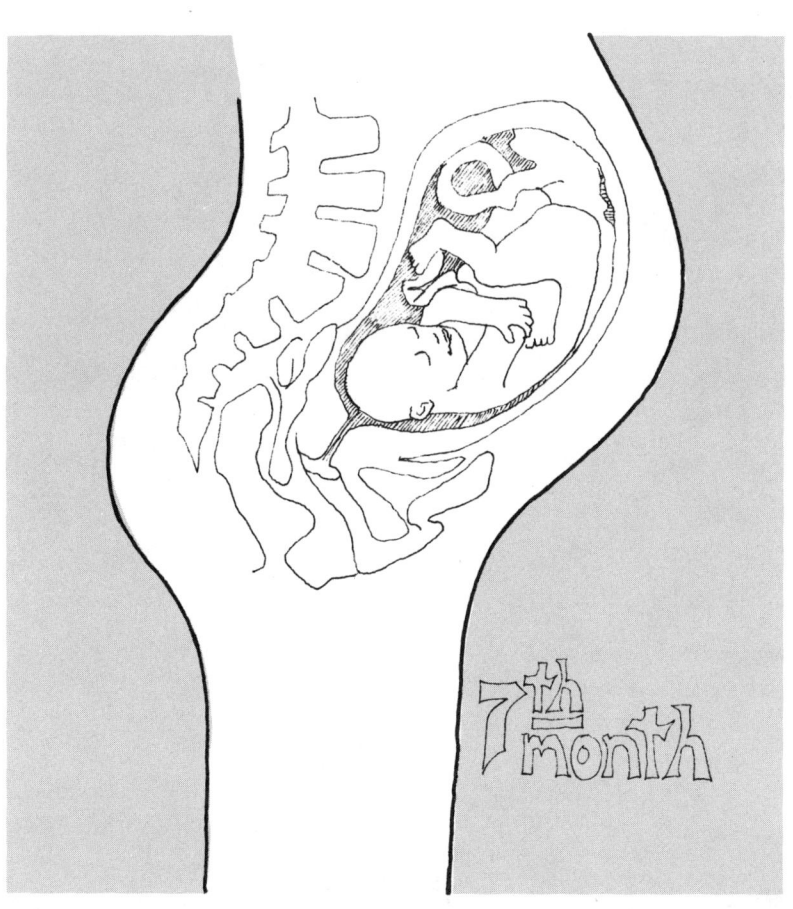

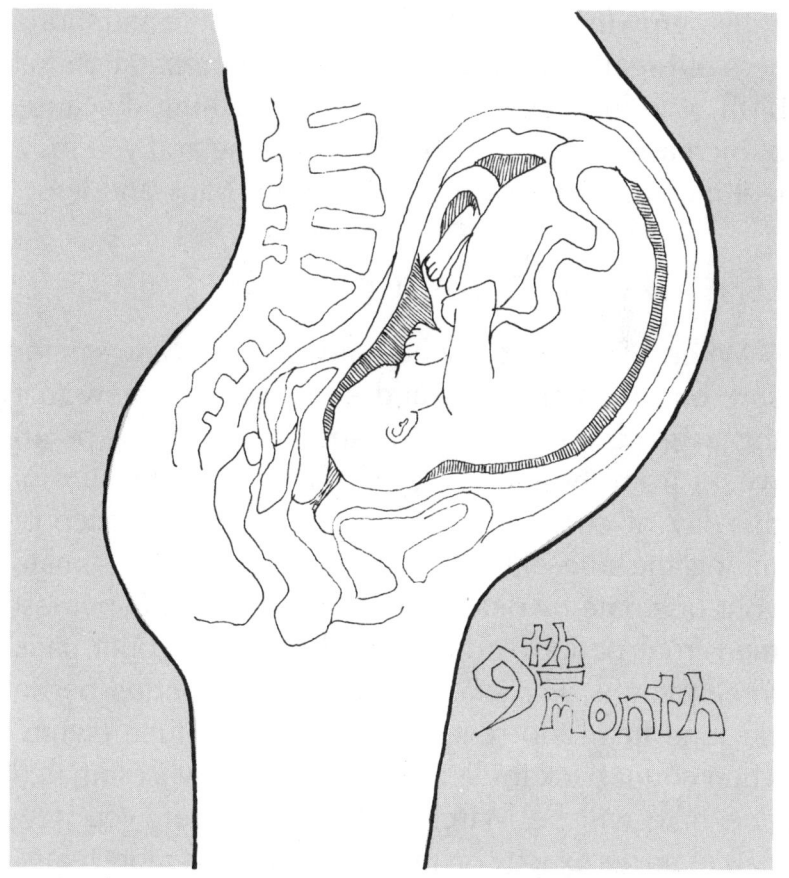

birth, you may have more aching joints. The added load may increase backache, and the stretching of your uterus may cause even more stretch marks. Because of the increased need for calcium, you may have muscle cramps. Nature may be getting you ready for motherhood as your sleep is interrupted by your baby's movements.

Ninth Month:

By now, you will really be ready for birth. Your baby's growth may cause increased pressure and shortness of breath. As your baby drops in preparation for birth, you may experience easier breathing. Because of increased weight, your feet may ache and you may feel increased pressure in your groin, back and legs.

LENGTH OF PREGNANCY

When will your baby be born? Nobody can say for sure but one can guess and estimate. We know that the average length of pregnancy is 280 days or 40 weeks from the time of ovulation. If you are sure of the day of conception you have a better chance of hitting the due date. If you don't, you can estimate your due date by determining the first day of your last menstrual period. Add seven days, then count back three months. For example, if your last period began on June first, add seven days, which is June eighth. Then count back three months. Your baby's estimated due date will be March eighth. However, very few babies arrive exactly on their due dates. It's more realistic to mark the period a week before and the week after. In fact, labor may be as much as three weeks before or two weeks after and still be within the normal range.

Advice From Amy

DEAR AMY:

I am one month pregnant and not only do I have morning sickness, but I have all day sickness. I am missing a lot of school and even when I'm there I can hardly concentrate on the work. Why am I so sick? Is there anything I can do about it? Does it hurt the baby?

Sickly Sue

DEAR SICKLY SUE,

Believe it or not, nausea is a good sign because it tells us that your baby is implanting well. If your nausea appears in the morning, the best time to prevent it is before getting out of bed. Place a dry cracker by your bed at night and take a few bites before rising in the morning. Avoid any sudden movements and get out of bed very slowly. Eat small amounts of food frequently throughout the day. Get plenty of fresh air. When you do have to vomit, a little ginger ale, soda water or sweet lemonade will give some relief. It may help you to know that this usually goes away after the twelfth week of pregnancy.

Amy

DEAR AMY:

I am two months pregnant and I have indigestion with everything I eat. Is this normal? I feel that everything I put down is going to come back up again. And when it does come back up I feel just awful. It's pretty hard to be in school and be sick all the time.

Funky Freida

DEAR FUNKY FREIDA,

During pregnancy, the hormones that keep your uterus from contracting (and expelling your baby) are also slowing down your digestion process. This will probably decrease in a few months and you will be able to eat again. To prevent indigestion try to get plenty of rest, fresh air and exercise. Eat small amounts of food rather than three large meals. Avoid rich, greasy foods, which can be upsetting. You may find it easier to keep down crackers, baked potatoes, toast and broiled foods. When you do have to throw up, try to relax and breathe slowly. DO NOT take over-the-counter drugs. These may hurt your baby. If the vomiting persists, call your doctor.

Amy

DEAR AMY:

I am in my second month of pregnancy and I notice a lot of mucous and discharge from my vagina. It doesn't really bother me but is it healthy? Should I call my doctor?

Concerned Carla

DEAR CONCERNED CARLA,

The mucous plug that seals your cervix (or the neck of your uterus) to prevent bacteria from harming your baby is now forming and that is why you see more mucous and discharge. If the discharge you experience is clear or milky and does not cause any irritation or unpleasant odor, it is probably natural. If the discharge becomes odorous, colored or irritating, there is probably an infection. Call your doctor.

Do watch out to keep this area clean because bacteria may form and cause infections (especially in the hot summer). Use only soap on the outside and rinse well. Do NOT douche.

Amy

DEAR AMY:

I'm two and a half months pregnant and I have to go to the bathroom all the time. It's kind of embarrassing at school and it even keeps me up all night. What can I do? Is this normal?

Bathroom Betty

DEAR BATHROOM BETTY,

Your need to urinate is a healthy sign. Don't try to prevent it or change it by drinking less water. For a healthy pregnancy, you must drink lots of liquids. Go to the bathroom every time you feel the need. To help you sleep at night, try drinking less in the evening and empty your bladder completely before going to bed. Any pain or burning during urination may tell you that you have a bladder or kidney infection. It's very important to contact your doctor if this happens.

Amy

DEAR AMY:

I am three months pregnant and I'm tired all the time. I used to go from morning until night and never stop. Now, with school and home and being pregnant, I don't know if I can get through the day. Sometimes I am so irritable with myself and my family that I can't stand myself. What can I do?

Crabby Carol

DEAR CRABBY CAROL,

Although fatigue is normal during pregnancy, it's probably twice as bad for teens. You've got school, homework, housework—and you're pregnant on top of that. It's pretty important that you do something about it, though, because fatigue can cause your baby to be born too early. It can also contribute to toxemia (a serious condition that you don't want!). There is no magic rule for the amount of sleep that you need. Try to go to bed earlier and rise later than usual. But extra sleep at night is not the only way you can help yourself. Try to include two daily rest periods (one of napping and one for relaxation).

Amy

DEAR AMY:

I used to laugh at TV ads about constipation, but now at 4 months pregnant, I don't think it's so funny. I haven't told anyone else about this problem, but I have a hard time going to the bathroom every day. Is this normal during pregnancy? I feel so full and gassy all the time (and I'm not too easy to live around either). What can I do?

DEAR CONSTIPATED CONNIE,

As your baby grows, the pressure of your uterus on the rectum may cause constipation. Drink three extra glasses of water a day in addition to your regular milk and juices. Make sure your diet contains whole grains, bran and whole wheat products. Eat fresh fruits, vegetables and salads every day to provide roughage. Establish a time each day for a regular bowel movement and never put off the urge. If constipation should occur, make it a point to drink three glasses of cool water at five minute intervals on rising. Then drink a glass of prune juice. Try to take raw bran, three times a day. Don't make a habit of laxatives and take them only when your doctor prescribes them.

Amy

DEAR AMY:

I am in my fifth month of pregnancy and though my nausea is gone, I feel a burning in my throat everytime I eat. My mother says I have heartburn and I'm just going to have to live with it. Is this so?

Heartburn Henrietta

DEAR HEARTBURN HENRIETTA,

As your uterus grows and presses upward, some of the contents of your stomach escape up into the tube that brings food to your stomach. To prevent heartburn, try to eat small frequent meals. Chew your food thoroughly and eat very slowly. Keep away from highly seasoned (no tacos), rich (no doughnuts), and fried or greasy foods (no French fries). Don't lie down right after eating. When you do suffer heartburn, try breathing in slowly and concentrate on relaxing. Do NOT take things like Alka Seltzer, sodium bicarbonate or baking soda because their high sodium (salt) content tends to promote water retention and swelling.

Amy

DEAR AMY:

I am six months pregnant and am horrified to find that I am getting "stretch marks." My mother says she got them too and there is nothing that I can do. Will I ever be able to wear a bikini again? Is there anything I can do to prevent it from getting worse?

Horrified Helen

DEAR HORRIFIED HELEN,

Unfortunately, your stretch marks are thought to come from your skin's inherited ability to stretch. So, as your mother says, they probably cannot be prevented or removed once they appear. While lotions may feel good and relieve itching, they probably do little to minimize stretch marks. However, some women do say that if you massage your stomach with cocoa butter, lanolin, or Vitamin E, you may help to minimize the marks. Try it, and I wish you luck. I might mention that the stretch marks will probably decrease considerably after birth.

Amy

DEAR AMY:

I have always had dark veins in my legs, but now that I am seven months pregnant I notice they are getting darker. Also, if I stand for long my legs get to feeling so restless and itchy that I can hardly bear it. Do you think I will get varicose veins? (My mother had them.) What are they and what can I do about them?

Varicose Vera

DEAR VARICOSE VERA,

As your uterus gets bigger, it tends to press on the major veins and they become stretched and swollen. To prevent varicose veins, it's important that you avoid standing for long periods of time. When sitting, raise your legs higher than your hips to relieve blood pooling. Exercise your feet and ankles in circles. Never sit with your feet or legs crossed. Above all, avoid constricting or tight clothing.

Amy

DEAR AMY:

Every time I get up I feel sharp, shooting pains at the bottom of my uterus. Sometimes I have to double over and wait for the pain to pass. Are these pains dangerous to me or to my baby?

Aching Aggie

DEAR ACHING AGGIE,

Your uterus is attached in your pubic area by ligaments whose job it is to keep the uterus in line. When your uterus grows, these ligaments stretch. Although the pain does not injure you or your baby, it can be uncomfortable. The pain usually appears when you sneeze, cough, laugh too hard, or more usually, when you get up too quickly. One of the best ways to prevent these pains is by moving slowly and carefully whenever you change positions. Turn carefully when you are in bed. If you feel twinges of pain in the groin, pull up your leg on the same side of the pain. Apply heat to the area with a hot water bottle or a warm cloth.

Amy

DEAR AMY:

My back hurts all the time. Now that I am eight months along it's getting worse than ever. I have a lot of pain down low. Will it get worse? What can I do to help myself?

Backache Betty

DEAR BACKACHE BETTY,

Pregnancy and backaches seem to go hand in hand. Backaches are usually the result of poor posture and muscle strain. Your back muscles are helping to support the extra weight of your uterus. What you can do to help is to concentrate on proper posture and exercise (See the chapter on exercise.). To help relieve backaches when you get them, put heat on your back and try to talk someone into giving you a back massage.

Amy

DEAR AMY:

Now that I am eight months pregnant, I have been getting these terrible spasms in my legs. I don't know when they are going to come, but when they do I have to stop everything and try to put up with the pain. They even wake me up at night and I have to jump out of bed. What can I do?

Crampy Chris

DEAR CRAMPY CHRIS,

This is just the month that your baby is storing more calcium than ever and is probably taking it from your system. Add more milk, cheese and Vitamin D to your diet. Drink plenty of fluids. Cramps can also be caused by the pressure of your uterus on the blood vessels to your legs. Avoid sudden stretching and change your position slowly and with care. Don't point your toes. When you do have a cramp, gently stretch your leg outward. Stroke gently in an up-and-down (not circular) direction. Try to put a hot water bottle on the cramps.

Amy

DEAR AMY:

This is my last month. I only have a few weeks to go, but I have difficulty in breathing. I feel that I just can't catch my breath. How long is this going to last and is there anything I can do about it?

Short of Breath Shelly

DEAR SHORT OF BREATH SHELLY,

Your uterus is pressing on your lungs, causing you difficulty in breathing and shortness of breath. You can sometimes make yourself more comfortable by standing straight up and giving your lungs more room for breathing. Sitting straight (and not slouching) also gives you more space in your chest. If you have trouble sleeping, prop yourself up with pillows so you can rest in a semi-sitting position. Practice deep breathing with your arms extended above your head. Toward the very end of your pregnancy your baby will probably "drop" or dip down into your pelvis (This is called lightening.) and will probably give you more room to breathe.

Amy

What Did You Do For Your Baby Today? (Nutrition and Exercise)

CHALLENGE:

One of the greatest challenges you teen moms have is to get the foods necessary for the proper growth and development for yourselves and your babies. Your nutritional needs are high as you have not yet reached your own full growth. These needs, added to those of your baby, call for special attention to what you eat. Your diet and exercise can help you feel and look better during your pregnancy.

CHOICE:

Every day you choose the foods for both you and your baby. You can choose empty-calorie junk foods or you (and only you) can choose foods that will give you and your baby all the extra nutrients and vitamins you need. You can also choose a regular exercise program that will help you adjust to the changes in pregnancy and help you make a speedy return to normal after your baby is born.

QUOTE:

"My major concern is that my baby is going to be healthy. I am worried about the possibility that my baby may not be healthy or he may be deformed. Because I had such a hard pregnancy I don't want to feel guilty or anything."

QUESTIONS:

How will eating right help me during pregnancy?
How will eating right help my baby to be born healthy?
Does my baby really eat what I eat?
What foods are good for my baby?
Are hamburgers healthy?
Does eating healthy mean I have to sacrifice my favorite foods?
Is it more expensive to buy all those healthy foods?
I like to snack after school. Are there any healthy foods I could snack on?
How can exercising help me in pregnancy?
When should I begin and how long should I exerercise?
Are there any exercises that will hurt me or my baby?
What exercises will help me look better?
What exercises will help me during birth?
What exercises will help me after the baby is born?
Why is relaxation important?
How can I get enough rest?

HOW WILL EATING RIGHT HELP ME DURING PREGNANCY?

Eating right will help you to:

- be healthier during pregnancy.
- look better during pregnancy.
- be stronger for labor and delivery.
- have a normal weight gain.
- handle your up and down moods better.
- get your figure back easier.

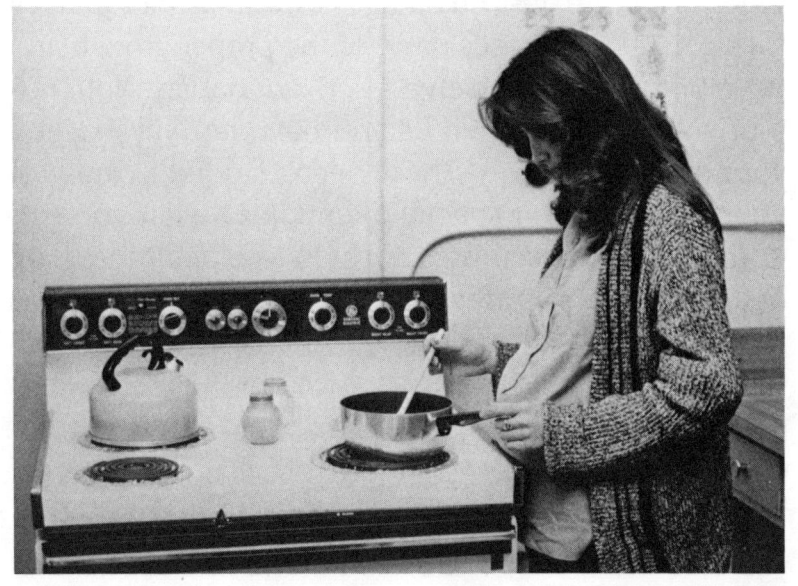

HOW WILL EATING RIGHT HELP MY BABY?

he food you take into your body contains the ONLY nutrients your baby gets. That is an awesome responsibility that no one else can share.

Eating right will help your baby to:
- be born healthy.
- have a well formed body.
- weigh a normal amount.
- be born on time.
- develop plenty of brain cells.
- have the best start in life.

DOES THE BABY REALLY EAT THE FOODS I EAT?

Your baby does not eat the foods in exactly the form you do. When you eat a hamburger your baby does not eat a hamburger; but, the nutrients from the food

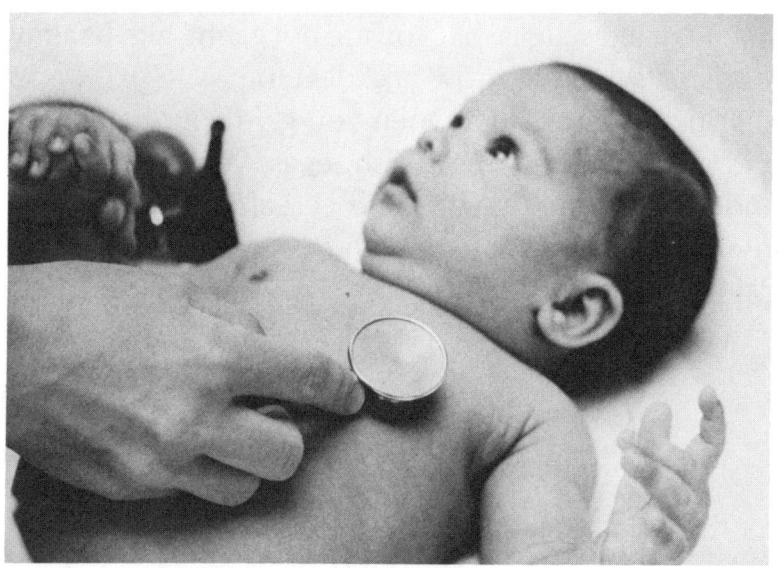

are passed into your blood stream to the placenta. The placenta changes the nutrients into just exactly the right form for your baby. If you eat poorly, your baby eats poorly. When you eat well, your baby eats well.

WHAT ARE THE FOODS THAT MY BABY NEEDS ME TO EAT?

When you are pregnant your need for calories increases only slightly. But, your need for foods rich in vitamins, minerals and nutrients *doubles*. Even if you are already getting good nutrition, now it has to be twice as good because you are eating nutrients (NOT CALORIES) for two. But how easy is that?

It's easy, if you start thinking of everything you eat in terms of, "What did I feed my baby today?"

You know only too well that when you feed your baby candy bars, soda pop, packaged cupcakes and sugar coated snacks that you are not giving him healthy foods on which to grow and develop.

You also know that when you give your baby milk and milk products, meat, fish, eggs, vegetables, fruits and whole wheat breads and cereals you have been giving him foods that are high in nutrients and low in calories.

FOODS HIGH IN NUTRIENTS AND LOW IN CALORIES

Let's look at each of these food groups and see what it does for both you and your baby. You will also see that you are already getting a lot of these foods.

Milk and Milk Products

What they do: Milk and milk products will give your baby the calcium he needs to build bones and teeth. At the same time they give you the vitamins you need for beautiful hair, skin and teeth, along with the calcium you need.

Where can you get them if you're not worried about calories?
Milkshakes, ice cream, puddings, custards, cheeseburgers.

Where can you get them if you are concerned with calories?
Skim milk, whole milk, yogurt, cheese.

Meat, Fish, Cheese, Eggs, Poultry, Beans, Peanut Butter and Nuts

What they do: Meat, fish, cheese, eggs, poultry, beans, peanut butter and nuts will give your baby the building blocks he needs to build cells for his body, brain and blood. They also give you the things you need to keep healthy and help you recover faster after delivery.

Where can you get them if you're not worried about calories?
Hamburgers, cheeseburgers, pizza, tacos, enchiladas, chili, chitlings, fried steak, fish, chicken, pork chops, nuts.

Where can you get them if you are concerned with calories?
Broiled steak, hamburgers, fish, chicken, peanut butter sandwiches, tuna fish salad.

Where can you get them if you're not worried about calories?
Whole wheat or enriched bread, rice, corn, tacos, grits, potatoes, pasta, noodles, macaroni, tortillas, muffins, dumplings, pancakes, waffles, cornbread, breakfast cereals (non-sweetened), oatmeal, cream of wheat.

Where can you get them if you are concerned about calories?
Be sure to get at least four servings a day of the above, but just don't gorge on them.

Breads And Cereals

What they do: Whole wheat or enriched breads and cereals provide your baby with important nutrients he is going to need for his heart and nervous system. They are importannt to you for healthy gums, teeth and blood vessels. They help your body make hemoglobin (a substance in your blood that helps you avoid anemia).

Fruits And Vegetables

What they do: Fruits and vegetables give you and your baby the vitamins and minerals you both need for healthy development of your teeth, gums, bones, and body cells. They play an important part in the development of your baby's skeleton, eyes and teeth, and they build resistance to infections.

Where to get them: Whether you are worried about calories or not, fruits and vegetables are your best friends. It is important to remember that only by eating a variety of fruits and vegetables can you and your baby receive all the necessary nutrients. Eat two or more servings of fruit a day: oranges, apples, grapefruit, watermelon, canteloupe, strawberries, etc. Eat two or more servings of vegetables a day: broccoli, cabbage, tomatoes, carrots, peas, mustard greens, pumpkin, etc. Dark green leafy vegetables are great for you.

WATER: Be sure to drink six to eight glasses of water each day to help your body use the food you eat and carry the wastes out of your body.

SPECIAL NEEDS

There are several nutrients, iron, calcium and folic acid, that are difficult to get in the amounts you need. Your doctor may prescribe vitamin tablets to supplement your diet.

DO I HAVE TO SACRIFICE MY FAVORITE FOODS?

If you don't have to be concerned about watching calories you don't have to sacrifice most of your favorite foods. If you are a potato chip addict or a cola addict, you may have to find replacements because these foods really give your baby nothing and give you nothing but greasy skin, greasy hair, fat and zits (none of which you want)!

BUT HOW CAN I THINK OF LIFE WITHOUT THESE?

We know that teens get almost half of their empty calories from snacks before, during and after school, in front of the TV. We also know that snacking is an important part of getting the nutrients you need. So, don't cut out snacking; simply replace the usual snack foods with cheese, meat, fruit or raw vegetables when you are thinking about pastries. For drinks you might try fruit juice or herb tea in place of soda pop. For dry snacks you might try unsalted popcorn in place of salty potato chips.

Fast Food and the Basic Four Food Groups

Food Group		MILK GROUP	MEAT GROUP	FRUIT-VEG. GROUP	GRAIN GROUP	"Others" Category
Recommended daily number of servings		3 for children 4 for teenagers 2 for adults	2 for all ages	4 for all ages	4 for all ages	none
Most important nutrients		calcium riboflavin (B_2) protein for strong bones and teeth, healthy skin, and good vision.	protein, niacin iron, thiamin (B_1) for muscle, bone, and blood cells, and healthy skin and nerves.	vitamin A, vitamin C to resist infections, heal wounds, and for night vision.	carbohydrate thiamin (B_1) iron, niacin for energy, and a healthy nervous system.	carbohydrate, fat These foods, low in most nutrients, are usually high in calories.
Fast food item	Number of calories	MILK GROUP	MEAT GROUP	FRUIT-VEG. GROUP	GRAIN GROUP	"Others" category
MAIN DISHES						
McDonald's®, Big Mac®	563	cheese	hamburger	onion, lettuce	roll	pickles, special sauce
Burger King®, Whopper®	670		hamburger	onions, lettuce, tomato	roll	catsup, pickles mayonnaise
Taco Bell®, beef taco	186	cheese	beef	lettuce	taco shell	
Taco Bell®, bean burrito	343	cheese	refried beans	onions	flour tortilla	sauce
Wendy's® chili	229		beans, beef	tomato sauce		
Dairy Queen®, chili dog	330		hot dog, beans	tomato sauce	roll	
Long John Silver's®, Fish/More®	894		fish	french fries, coleslaw	hush puppies	
Arby's®, Ham'N Cheese®	380	cheese	ham	lettuce, tomato	roll	
Kentucky Fried Chicken® dinner	643		chicken	mashed potatoes, coleslaw	roll	gravy
McDonald's®, Egg McMuffin®	327	cheese	egg, canadian bacon		english muffin	
Pizza Hut®, pork and mushroom pizza	380	cheese	pork	mushrooms, tomato sauce	crust	
DESSERTS						
Dairy Queen®, banana split	540	ice cream	nuts	banana		whipped cream, strawberry topping, pineapple topping, chocolate syrup
Dairy Queen®, ice cream cone	150	ice cream				cone
other desserts	240-250					pies, cookies, turnovers, danish pastry
SIDE DISHES (calories)				french fries (220) coleslaw (121) corn on the cob (169) mashed potatoes (64)	roll (61) hush puppies (153)	onion rings (270) gravy (23)
BEVERAGES (calories)		whole milk (150) 2% milk (120) McDonald's® chocolate shake (383)		orange juice (80)		McDonald's® soft drinks (144) coffee (2)

©1983, National Dairy Council, Rosemont, IL 60018. All rights reserved.

AREN'T ALL THOSE FOODS EXPENSIVE?

Compare the costs of empty calorie foods with healthy foods. You'll find that dollar for dollar you get twice as much for your money when you buy healthy foods.

GREAT PROTEIN SNACKS
Tuna fish sandwich
Fried chicken
Chili
Tacos filled with meat, tomatoe and cheese
Peanut butter sandwich
Beef and vegetable stew
Rice and Bean casserole
Hamburgers
Cheeseburgers
Grilled cheese sandwiches

These are all excellent brain and body food for the baby because they are all high in protein.

REMINDERS: JUNK FOODS & EMPTY CALORIES

GOOEY food loaded with empty calories fills you up and out but it doesn't give you what your body and your baby need.

Try cheese, meat, fruit, and raw vegetables in place of pastries.
Try fruit juice or water in place of soda pop.
Try unsalted popcorn in place of salty potato chips.

Nutrient-rich foods give you shining hair, smooth skin, bright eyes, and a slimmer figure.
Calorie-rich foods give you greasy hair, zits and fat.

Empty calories (candy bars, soda, packaged cupcakes and sugar-coated snacks and nibbles) turn right into fat without real nourishment.

When you are hungry, grab some fresh fruit, yogurt, raisins, nuts, a piece of swiss cheese or a peanut butter sandwich or some raw carrots.

HOW CAN EXERCISING HELP ME?

The small amount of time that you put into exercise can help you in many ways. It can:

- help you feel better during pregnancy.
- help you look better during pregnancy.
- help relieve many of the stresses of pregnancy.
- help you prepare for childbirth.
- help you return to normal more quickly after birth.

WHEN SHOULD I BEGIN AND HOW LONG SHOULD I EXERCISE?

Begin exercising seriously from the beginning of your pregnancy to prevent many of the minor discomforts from ever beginning. You will need to practice every day for twenty minutes. You might want to schedule your time for ten minutes in the morning before school and ten minutes in the evening (before bedtime).

ARE THERE ANY EXERCISES THAT WILL HURT ME OR MY BABY?

Most of the exercises you do now you can continue until your baby's birth. Especially good exercises are swimming, walking, and hiking. Jogging or horseback riding will probably become too uncomfortable to continue up through your ninth month. Let comfort be your guide.

WHERE AM I GOING TO FIND TIME FOR MY EXERCISES?

Every person has a time that is best for her. Try to think of ten or twenty minutes each day that would be the most attractive. It might be when you get up, or when you go to bed. Listening to music or watching your favorite TV show for twenty or thirty minutes will make your exercise time pass by quickly.

WHAT IS THE MOST IMPORTANT EXERCISE I CAN DO?

Probably the most important exercise that you can learn during pregnancy (and continue the rest of your life) is good posture. WHY?

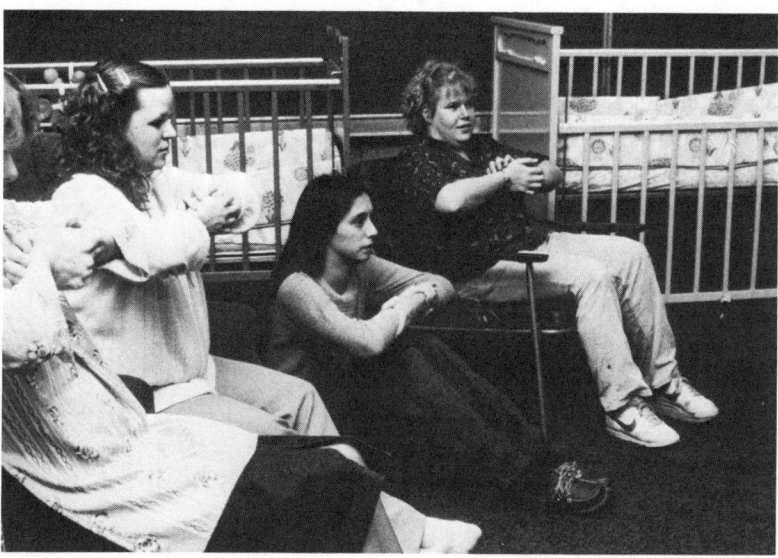

Poor posture:
- causes strain on your joints and muscles.
- causes backaches.
- makes you look fat.
- makes you look swayback.
- makes breathing more difficult.

Think of yourself as a puppet on a string:

1. Tuck in your buttocks.
2. Tilt your pelvis back. Pretend it is a bowl and you are keeping the contents from spilling out.
3. Straighten your spine.
4. Pull your shoulders back comfortably with your arms relaxed at your sides.
5. Pretend that a string is at the top of your head and gently pull up. Think tall!
6. Keep your head erect with your chin tucked in.

Make this a habit for the rest of your life!

HOW TO PICK UP SOMETHING

To avoid back strain when picking up something from the floor:

1. Always squat.
2. Keep your back straight.
3. Bring the object close to your body.
4. Rise, using your leg muscles to lift.
5. Never bend forward with your knees straight.

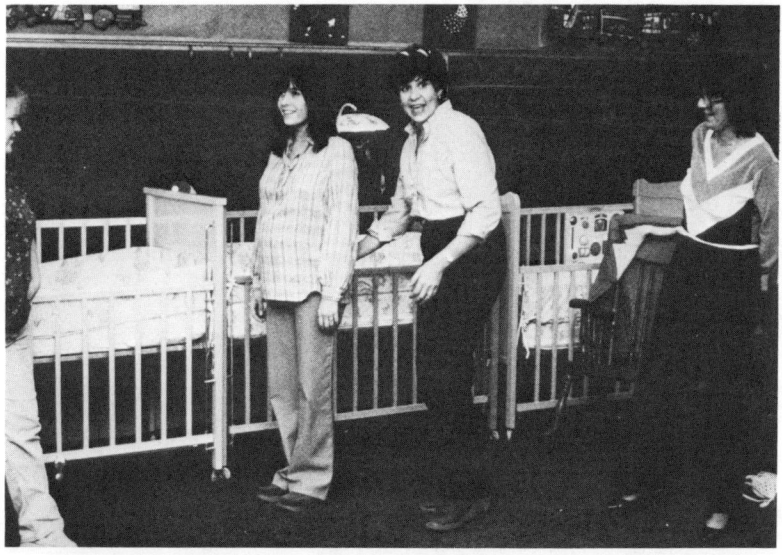

HOW TO CHANGE POSITIONS

Sudden change in position can cause severe strain of your abdominal muscles and your back muscles. It can also cause dizziness and muscle cramps.

To get up from lying down:

1. Turn on your side (if you are lying on your back).
2. Bend your knees up.
3. Gently push yourself up with your arms.

(Reverse the movements to lie down.)

WHAT IS A GOOD EXERCISE FOR MY BACK AND TUMMY?

The next most important exercise you can learn for pregnancy (and the rest of your life) is an exercise that strengthens your back muscles and your abdominal muscles and is essential to good posture. It's called the pelvic tilt.

THE PELVIC TILT

Think of your pelvis as a bowl. This bowl can swing forward or backward on your spine. Now think of your baby as the contents of that bowl. Swing the bowl forward tipping your baby out. Now swing the bowl backward and pull your baby back in. This is the pelvic tilt (and is just what belly dancers do!). As your baby gets bigger, your uterus tends to swing your pelvis forward, causing your spine to curve. And, of course, this is why you get your backache. You can prevent backache (or at least make it less uncomfortable) by practicing these six steps:

1. Stand normally.
2. Pull in your buttocks.
3. Tuck in your abdominal muscles.
4. Straighten your spine.
5. Pull the top of the bowl backward (holding your baby in). Hold it.   6. Release.

Pelvic tilt—lying down

1. Lie on your back with both knees bent and your feet flat on the floor.
2. Now tip the bowl backward by pressing the small of your back against the floor. (Pull your baby in).

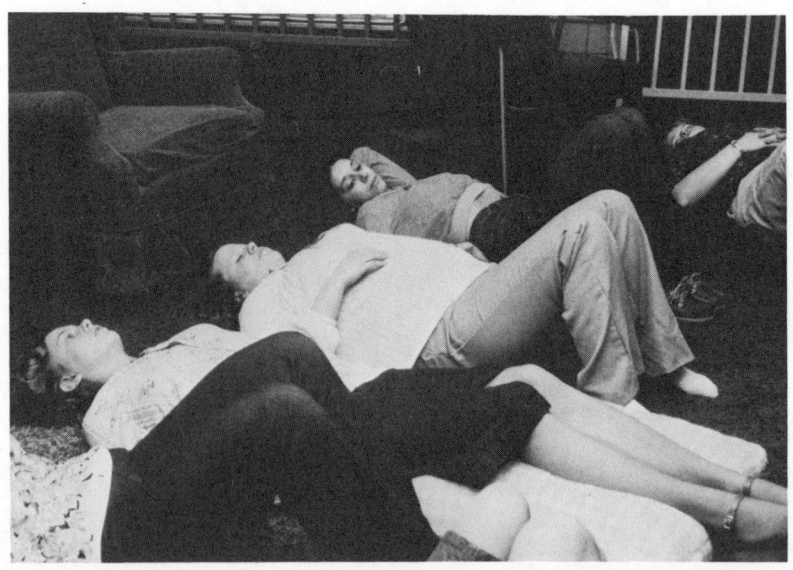

3. Tighten your abdominal muscles.
4. Hold for four counts and release.

Pelvic tilt—on hands and knees

1. Get on your hands and knees as if you were scrubbing the floor.
2. Now pull in your buttocks.
3. Round your shoulders and press your chin on your chest.
4. Tip the bowl back as if you were pulling your baby in.
5. Slightly arch your back.
6. Hold for four counts and release.

WHAT EXERCISE WILL KEEP MY TUMMY FIRM?

You are probably concerned with the state of your tummy muscles. Do this exercise both before and after the birth of your baby.

1. Lie on the floor with your legs bent and feet flat.
2. With your arms behind your head, tilt your pelvis, keeping your back flat against the floor.
3. Slowly curl your head and shoulders forward and reach toward your knees as far as you can comfortably go.
4. Hold and release.

WHAT EXERCISE WILL HELP MY LEGS AND THIGHS?

To keep your legs and thighs from becoming fatigued and cramped, try this:

1. Lie on your back, knees bent, feet flat on floor.
2. Tilt your pelvis.
3. Breathe in slowly as you raise one leg and straighten it.
4. Breathe out slowly as you lower your leg to the floor.
5. Bring leg back to bent position and repeat with other leg.

WHAT EXERCISE WILL HELP MY FEET FROM SWELLING?

While sitting or lying down, try these movements:

1. Slowly rotate your ankles in a full wide circle to the right.
2. Then rotate them to the left.

IS THERE ANY EXERCISE THAT WILL HELP MY SHORTNESS OF BREATH?

Shortness of breath comes from not having any room to breathe in your later months. This exercise will give you more room:

1. Sit or stand with arms at side.
2. Bend your elbows so that your fingertips rest on your shoulders.
3. Keeping your body erect, inhale deeply and slowly stretch your right arm upward.
4. As you breathe out, slowly lower your arm.
5. Repeat with your left arm.
6. Then do it with both arms—stretching, stretching, stretching.

WHAT EXERCISES WILL HELP ME DURING BIRTH?

During birth you are going to have to push your baby out through the vaginal opening. This is going to take a combination of pushing with your abdominal muscles, stretching your thighs, and relaxing your pelvic floor. If it sounds complicated, don't worry. Just do each of these three exercises and you will be in good shape.

Abdominal Push

1. Take a deep breath and slowly blow it out.
2. Keep blowing and blowing (Don't breathe in.). Pretend there is a candle there that you have to blow out.
3. As you keep blowing (Don't let up!), you will begin to feel your abdominal muscles pouch out. These are the muscles you will use to bear down during delivery.

Thigh Stretch

1. Sit on the floor with one leg bent in front of you and the other leg stretched out straight.
2. Slowly and gently bend forward at your hip and reach with your arms to your foot. Try to touch your toes.
3. Hold and relax.
4. Do it with the other foot.

Pelvic Floor Muscles Control

This exercise is important for birth and after when you are trying to recover. As your baby comes out of the vagina, he/she will naturally stretch all those muscles. It is important that you learn to control this area.

1. Push as if to urinate.
2. Now stop the flow by pulling your muscles in.
3. If you can't get the feeling, next time you are on the toilet urinating, stop the flow and concentrate on those muscles you have to use.

REST AND SLEEP

Rest and sleep are times for your body to restore. For a healthy pregnancy it is very important for you to avoid becoming excessively tired. This is especially difficult when you have a full day of school on top of being pregnant. Take out time each day (maybe before or after your exercises) to relax. Try to take a nap during the afternoon, maybe after school. Try to go to bed earlier and get up later. Although different women need different amounts of sleep, you should have enough sleep and rest to prevent ending the day exhausted and irritable.

Prenatal Care For You And Your Baby

CHALLENGE:

When you are a pregnant teen, your baby has a higher risk of being born too early and too small. As a teen mom, you yourself have a greater risk of toxemia, miscarriage and stillbirth.

CHOICES:

Getting early care means you provide protection for your baby so that he or she will not be born too small or too soon.

QUOTE:

"My biggest concern was my health. I had terrible swelling in my hands, feet and face, and I was tired all the time. My doctor said it was toxemia and I had to stay in bed. He told me that it could be dangerous to both me and my baby."

QUESTIONS:

What do they do during a prenatal exam?
Will the doctor make me undress?
Will they examine my vagina?
Will it hurt?
What kinds of questions will they ask me?
Can they tell how pregnant I am?

THE PRENATAL EXAM

 Your prenatal exam will be in three parts. The first part is to examine how you, *the mother*, are doing. The second part is to examine *the passageway* through which your baby will pass, and the third part is to see how your *baby* is doing.

GENERAL EXAM

They didn't ask me to undress at first. They sat me down and asked me a lot of questions about the kind of food I eat, my work, and my schooling. They asked me questions about my family and any illnesses that had been in my family. They asked me if I had had any illnesses or operations and if I use any drugs or have had any problems in the past. I was then asked if I could remember my last menstrual period and how long my periods usually lasted. They weighed me and told me that I wasn't to worry about my weight and that it was important that I ate good foods so that my baby would be born healthy. They said I would gain anywhere from 24 to 34 pounds and that most of that would be in the last three months of my pregnancy.

URINE SAMPLE

Then they asked me to go into the bathroom and to give them a urine sample in a little paper cup. They told me that my urine could tell them if my kidneys were functioning like they should.

BLOOD SAMPLE

They took a needle and poked it into my skin. Although it didn't feel good, it didn't really hurt. They told me that my blood could tell them many important things like my blood type (just in case I needed a blood transfusion at birth). It tells them if I am Rh positive or negative. And it tells them if I have enough iron in my blood.

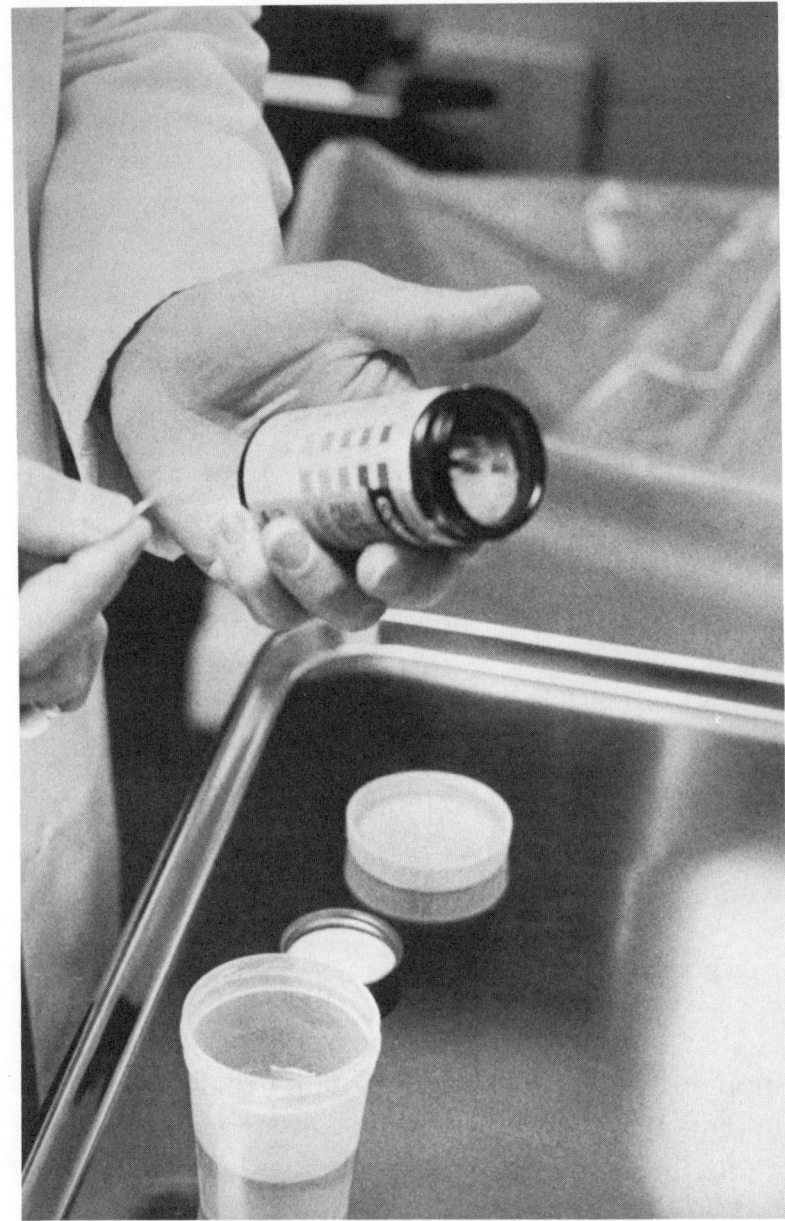
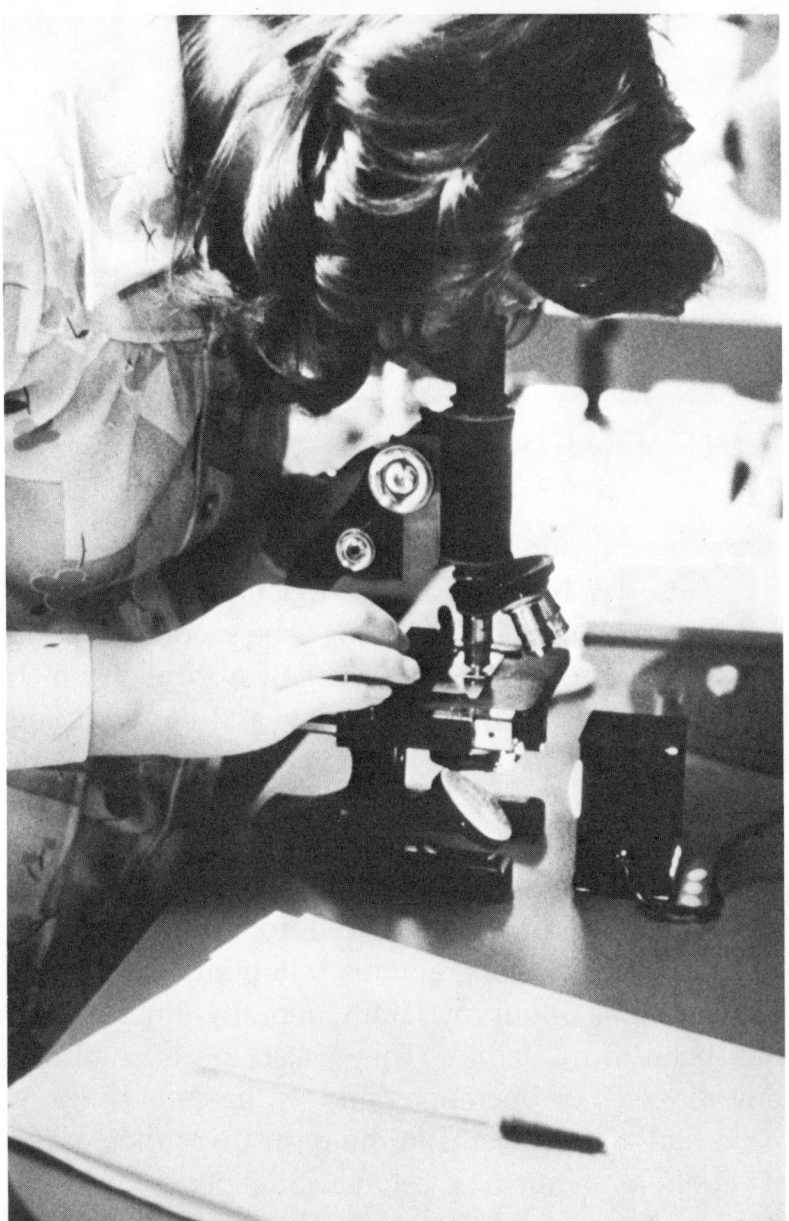

BLOOD PRESSURE

Then they put a band around my arm to take my blood pressure. They said that if my blood pressure was high it would close down the vessels that take blood to my baby. They explained that they could tell if I had something called toxemia which would also endanger my baby. They explained that good nutrition and lots of rest and healthy exercise could keep my blood pressure down.

OBSTETRICAL EXAM

Then they asked me to get undressed. The doctor was going to examine my uterus, cervix and vagina to get some idea of what kind of birth I would have. This is the part of the exam I was so afraid of—undressing in front of strangers and having something put into my vagina. Ugh! But the nurse was very gentle with me, and I had a gown so I never was undressed. The doctor then told me everything he was going to do. He told me that if I relaxed and took deep breaths, nothing would hurt. He said that if I tensed up, it probably would hurt. Well, I had nothing to lose so I closed my eyes and concentrated on relaxing.

VULVA: I lay back on a table and put my legs in supports. The doctor told me he was examining the outside for inflammation, sores or color changes. I didn't feel anything. Then he told me he was going to put two fingers of his gloved hand inside my vagina.

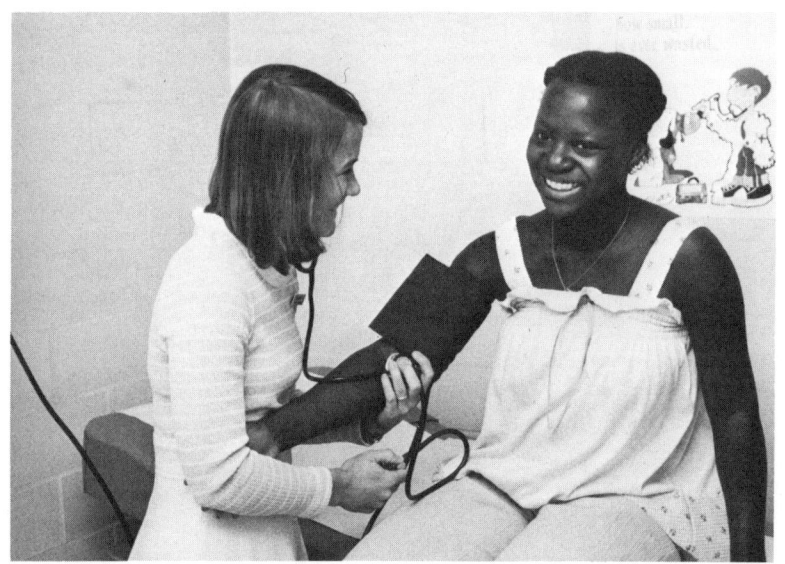

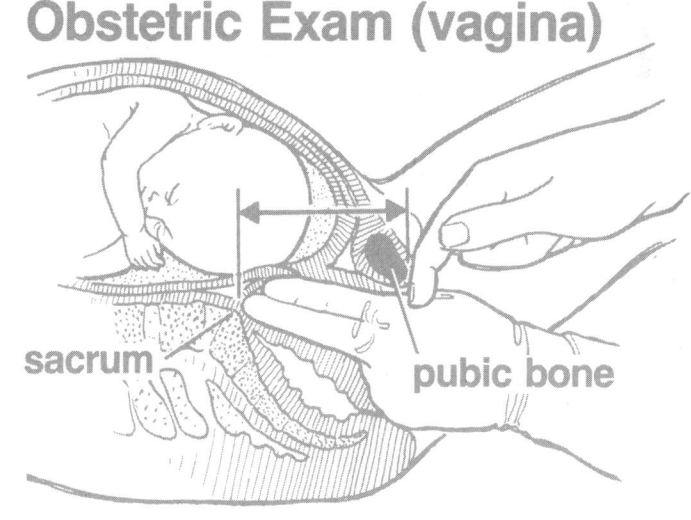

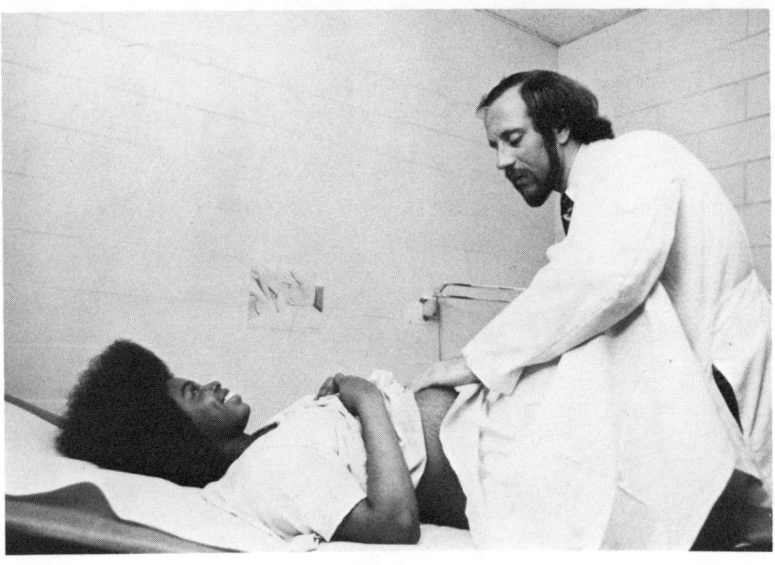

Obstetric Exam (pelvis)

Again he told me it wouldn't hurt if I didn't tense up. I concentrated on relaxing and breathing deeply and hardly felt his fingers go in.

UTERUS: He put one hand on the outside of my abdomen and moved my uterus from side to side. He said that he was trying to guess the size of my uterus and that would tell him how pregnant I was.

VAGINA: Then he put in a plastic instrument. He told me he had warmed and put lubrication on the instrument so it wouldn't hurt me. I felt it slip in and then he told me that he was going to open it a little bit to look at the vagina (or the birth canal down which my baby would come). He said also that he was going to look at the cervix (or neck of the uterus). The color and feel of this would tell him about how far along I was.

PELVIS: He then felt inside for the size of my bones (or pelvic measurements), which would tell him how big I was and what kind of a labor I might have. He said it was too early to tell the size of my baby but by the end of my pregnancy we could probably get some idea if I was big enough to have an easy labor.

They listened to my heart because they said that my baby would increase my blood volume by almost half and that it was a greater stress on my whole system.

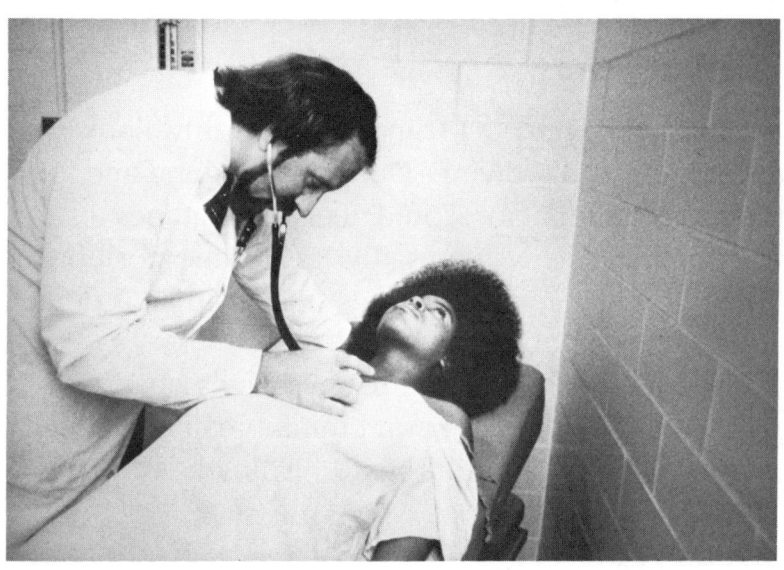

BREAST AND NIPPLES

They examined my breasts and nipples and said that if I were going to breastfeed my baby, I would need some kind of preparation.

GUMS AND TEETH

They looked at my gums and teeth. The doctor said that it was especially important that I take good care of my teeth. They warned me not to get any x-rays from the dentist.

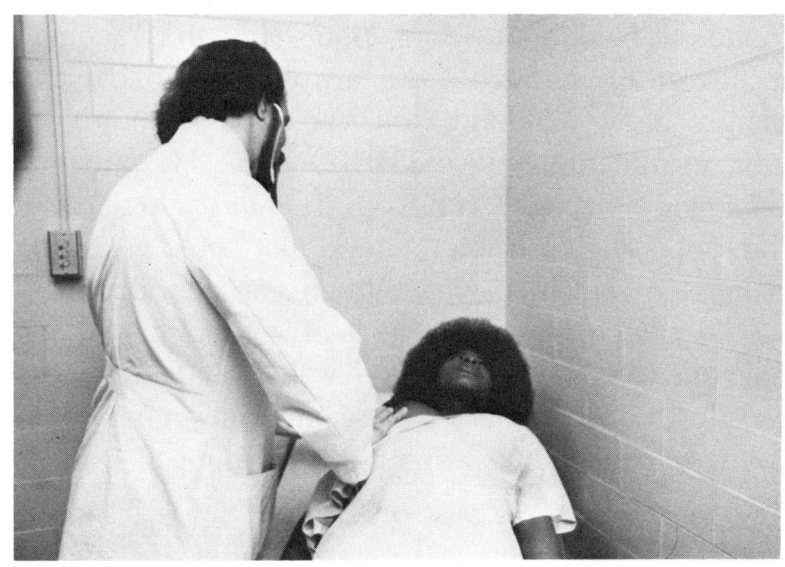

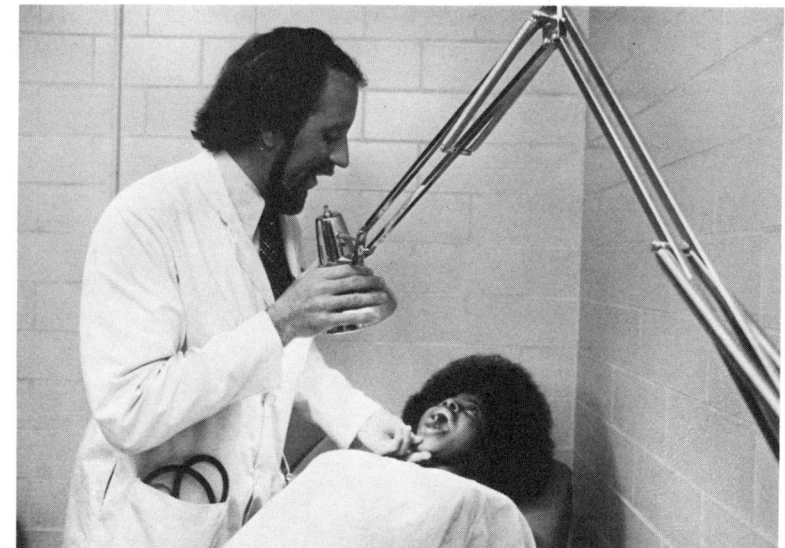

Obstetric Exam (abdomen)

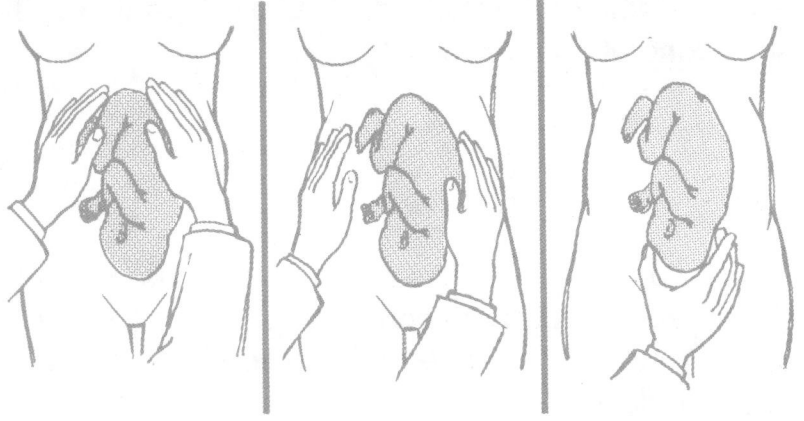

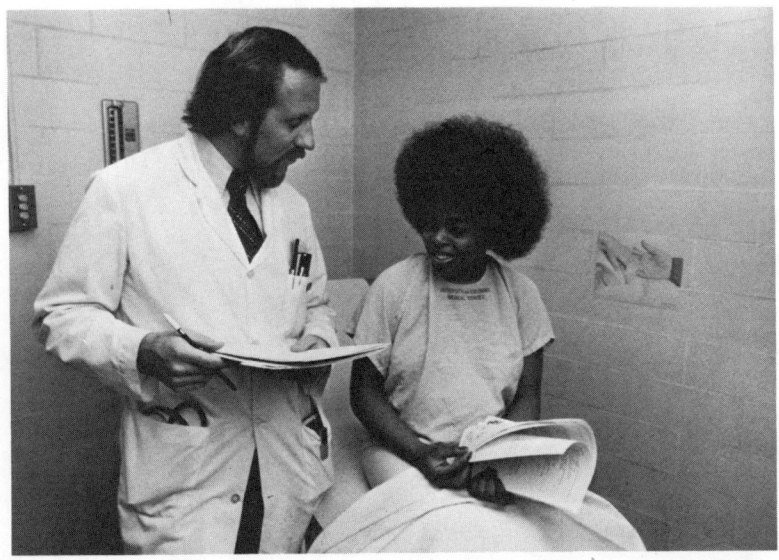

FETAL EXAM

Next they wanted to find out how my baby was developing and growing. During the second and third trimester, the doctor could feel the outlines of my baby's body in my uterus. By feeling the position of his buttocks, back, arms, legs and head, the doctor could tell a lot about my baby.

Finally, we got to listen to my baby's heartbeat. It was worth everything! I don't think I really believed a baby was in there until I heard his tiny heartbeat.

FOLLOWUP

Then the doctor told me to get dressed and come into his office where we could talk about what he found. He said that I was in good shape, that I seemed to have a big enough passageway for my baby, and that my baby was doing well. We discussed nutrition, and he told me again NOT TO DIET. He said that pregnancy was NOT THE TIME TO DIET. He said that the food I ate was the only food that could get to my baby. He said that even though I ate good food, I would need extra supplements of iron, folic acid and calcium. He gave me some vitamins to take with me. Finally, he asked me if I had some questions—and I did. I wanted to know about a lot of things!

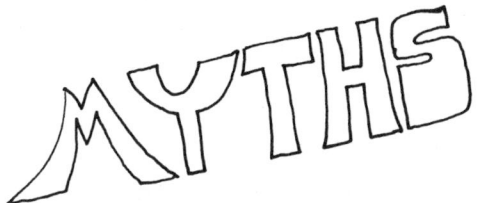

YOUR DOCTOR CAN HELP DISPEL ANY MYTHS THAT YOU HAVE HEARD AND THAT HAVE FRIGHTENED YOU.

MYTH: If you look at something ugly or frightening, your baby will be deformed.

TRUTH: Nothing you look at can deform your baby. But drugs, smoking, alcohol and poor nutrition can harm your baby.

MYTH: You shouldn't reach over your head because the umbilical cord will strangle your baby.

TRUTH: Your baby floats around in a sac of fluid. The umbilical cord is always full like a garden hose and your reaching can't affect it.

MYTH: If you eat strawberries, wine, grapes, etc., your baby will have birthmarks.

TRUTH: Nothing you eat can cause birthmarks. They are caused by an abnormal condition of the blood vessels in the skin.

MYTH: You shouldn't eat a lot of food because you will become fat.

TRUTH: You should eat a lot of meat, fish, fruits, vegetables, cereals, and dairy products so you can have a big, healthy baby.

THE MOST COMMON QUESTIONS WE WANTED TO ASK OUR DOCTORS

HOW BAD IS SMOKING FOR MY BABY?

When you smoke, your baby does too. Smoking causes your blood vessels to contract, so your baby gets less blood. His heart has to beat faster. He will probably weigh less and get a poorer start in life. Try

to stop smoking. If you can't, at least try to limit the number of cigarettes you (and your baby) smoke each day. Avoid inhaling smoke from others who smoke around you because your baby gets even that.

MY FAMILY IS GOING AWAY ON A TRIP. CAN I TRAVEL WITH THEM?

Traveling is okay. If you go by car be sure to stop for a walk every two hours. Wear loose clothing. If you travel by plane, train or bus, be sure to get up and move around often. Don't sit with your legs crossed.

HOW BAD IS ALCOHOL FOR MY BABY?

When you drink, your baby drinks too. Unfortunately your baby is affected more because he is so small. Alcohol can have serious effects. Babies with fetal alcohol syndrome never catch up to normal physical and emotional growth.

I HAVE TO GO TO THE DENTIST. WHAT ABOUT GETTING X-RAYS?

X-rays, especially during early pregnancy, can damage your baby. From the time you first suspect that you are pregnant, be sure to let any doctor or dentist know. There should be absolutely no x-rays during pregnancy because your developing baby is susceptible to radiation damage.

CAN I TAKE MEDICATIONS FOR A HEADACHE?

From the day of conception your developing baby is vulnerable to any chemical substance.

His development is especially vulnerable during the first one hundred days when his organs are being formed. Since you may be unaware you are pregnant for several weeks or even months, you should be especially careful with medication. When you are pregnant, it's important not to take unprescribed drugs. This includes all aspirin, reducing aids, nose drops, douches, ointments, laxatives, etc.

I NOTICE THAT MY GUMS ARE BLEEDING AND SORE. WHAT CAN I DO?

If you have been nauseated, had heartburn or other problems, you may not have been taking good care of your gums and may not have received good nutrition.

Brush and floss your teeth everyday. Visit your dentist—but don't get any x-rays until after your baby is born.

CAN MARIJUANA OR DRUGS HURT MY BABY?

When you smoke marijuana or take drugs such as heroin, cocaine and amphetamines, you pass the drugs directly to your baby. These drugs are especially dangerous and your baby can even become addicted before birth.

I HEAR THAT SPRAY CANS CAN BE DANGEROUS. IS THIS TRUE?

Fumes from aerosol spray cans, pesticides and chemicals can be inhaled and passed on to your baby. Avoid spray cans as much as possible.

WHAT ELSE SHOULD I KNOW?

- Keep away from partially cooked meat.
- Don't empty or be around your cat's litter box.
- Stay away from anyone who is ill while you are pregnant. Avoid all contagious diseases such as measles, chicken pox, diptheria, polio, flu, mumps and smallpox. If you have been near a person with any disease, call your doctor at once. Blood tests will tell if you are susceptible and there are now vaccines that will counteract your exposure.
- Stay away from anyone who has rubella or German measles. It is known to cause birth defects in babies and will have tragic effects on your baby. Call your doctor if you have been exposed to anyone with this disease.
- If you have been exposed to herpes or have it, it can affect your baby both during its development and on the way down your birth canal during childbirth. Tell your doctor about your exposure.
- Stay away from any personal contact with anyone who has a sexually transmitted disease (such as VD). These diseases can have tragic effects on your baby.

WHEN TO CALL YOUR DOCTOR

You have every reason to look forward to a healthy pregnancy and a normal delivery. However, things can and do happen—and that's why you have a doctor.

Don't hesitate to call your doctor or your clinic if you experience any of these symptoms that signal that either you or your baby may be in danger.

- Vaginal bleeding
- Severe abdominal pain
- Swelling of your face, feet or hands
- Dimness or blurring of vison
- Persistent vomiting
- Chills and fever
- Sudden escape of fluid from your vagina

With your doctor's attention and care, any of these problems can be taken care of.

From Laughter To Tears: Emotional And Social Changes

CHALLENGE:

Even when you are not pregnant, being a teen is a stressful time. The major problems of teens today are tension and depression. Add pregnancy, boyfriends, husbands and school to that!

CHOICE:

Stress is not all bad—it can be motivating, maturing and a learning experience, if you can get support from your family, your friends, your community and your school.

QUOTE:

"I feel I am so pressured sometimes that I just blow up. It's so much pressure…twenty-four hours a day, every day. And you don't get a break. It's really hard to cope with."

QUESTIONS:

Why am I so emotional?
Why am I so nice one minute and mean the next?
How can I tell my boyfriend I'm pregnant?
How can I tell my parents?
How can I cope with my feelings?
Why is there so much stress in the teen years?
Where can I get help?
How can I find a support system?
What if I don't have a husband or boyfriend?
What if my parents won't support me?

WHY IS THERE SO MUCH STRESS IN THE TEEN YEARS?

ven before we got pregnant we were having stress in our lives. There was stress at school. We had homework, classes and teachers to deal with. We had problems with friends and especially boyfriends. On top of that there was pressure to drink, to use drugs and do what our friends were doing, whether we wanted to or not.

A lot of our own parents were going through their own stressful times. When they were fighting, we just wanted to get away. When they were getting divorced, we had problems living with our families. And then we had problems with stepparents, stepbrothers and sisters and all that mess.

It seems as if there is no one to listen to us. Our parents seem to have forgotten they had problems when they were teens themselves. They want us to be perfect students and perfect people, even though they know that they had gotten in trouble themselves when they were teens.

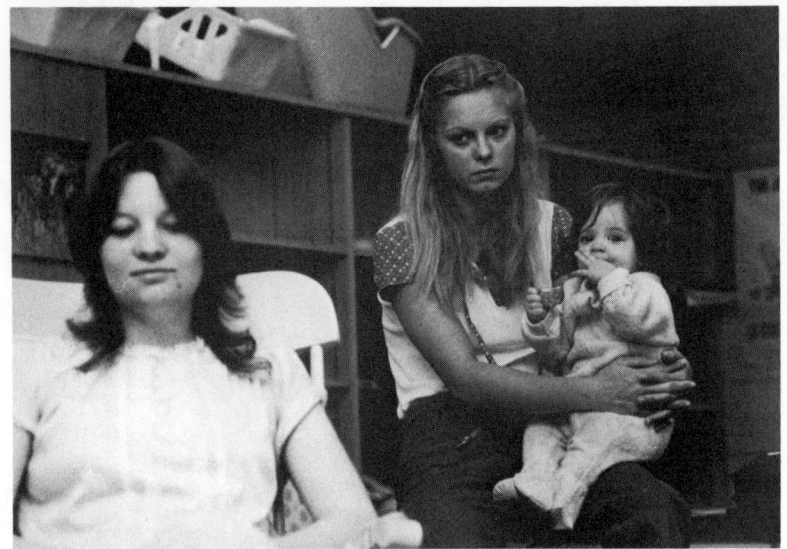

There's and old saying about pregnancy that often describes the changing emotional states quite well:

> Three months dreary
> Three months cheery
> Three months weary

You will find that your pregnancy falls into three major periods: The first three months (1-3) is called your first trimester. The second three months (4-6) is called your second trimester. The third three months (7-9) is called your last trimester of pregnancy.

FIRST TRIMESTER CHANGES:

Many of us found the first trimester our most trying one. When we first realized we were pregnant, we had a lot of worries. Not only were we worried about pregnancy, childbirth and parenting, but, because most of us hadn't planned the birth, the news that we were pregnant was *very* upsetting.

Most of us couldn't believe we were pregnant and tried to cover it up for as long as we could. We were so depressed we could hardly get through the day. Our big question was what to do next. How should we tell our boyfriends (if we had boyfriends)? What would they say? Would the fathers of the babies stick by us? How should we tell our parents? What should we say to our friends? What should we tell the school?

Now, put pregnancy on top of that!

Add the stress of telling your boyfriend you are pregnant and not knowing what he is going to say. Plus having to tell your parents and knowing they are going to be mad or disappointed. Throw in having your friends find out and having them make fun of you or shun you. Plus having to leave school, being sick in the morning, getting fat, growing out of your clothes, being tired all the time. It's not a fun time!

WHY AM I SO EMOTIONAL?

Try to relax and don't worry. Pregnancy is a time of emotions and your ups and downs are all part of nature's plan to help you through your journey from a single person to a parent.

Should we get abortions, continue the pregnancies, bear our children, keep the children, get married, leave town, or give our babies up?

Emotional Changes

SHOCK: *I couldn't believe it was me. I wouldn't believe I was pregnant and going to have a baby—I was nothing but a baby myself.*

DENIAL: *Well, I just didn't admit it. I pretended that nothing was different. Even when I threw up every morning I kept telling my mom it was something I ate.*

ANGER: *When I told my boyfriend I was pregnant he told me he wasn't the father, even though he knew I had never been with another boy. I was mad at him, mad at myself, mad at my mother and mad at the world.*

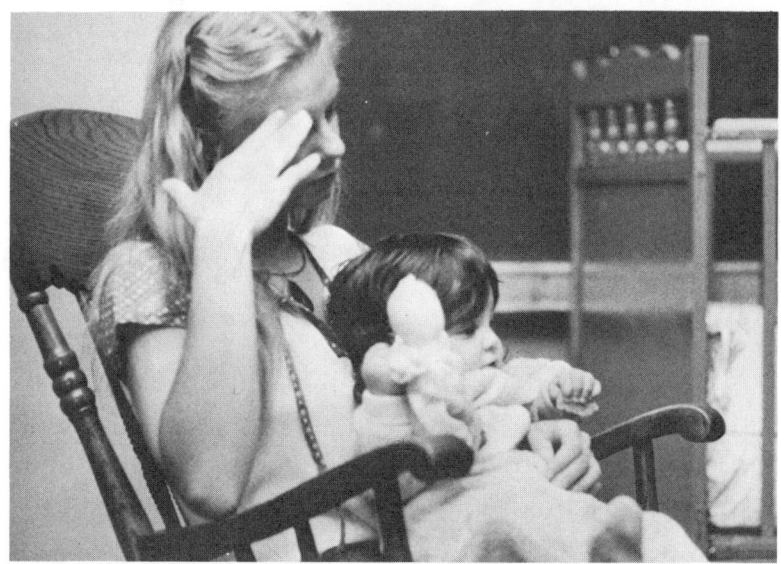

BARGAINING: *I wanted my boyfriend to marry me. He said he'd pay for an abortion, but he wouldn't marry me. Then he agreed to marry me but my parents were against it. Finally I promised my parents that I would finish school if they let me marry my boyfriend. Then he didn't want to marry me. It was a mess.*

SELF PITY; SUFFERING: *I felt like my life was ruined. Why did God pick me to suffer? I kept thinking how great my life was before the pregnancy.*

CONFUSION: *I couldn't decide if I should keep my baby. All my friends told me that an abortion would be best for me and my baby. The baby's father told me he would pay for the abortion. My mother did not want me to have an abortion for religious reasons and my father wouldn't even speak to me. I couldn't think straight.*

HAPPINESS: *Well, I was very happy—and so was my husband. I had always wanted a baby, and, after my parents' divorce, I wanted someone for me to love and someone to love me. I've had lots of sisters and brothers and I really love babies. My husband is happy too.*

CREATIVITY: *I've never felt so creative in my life. To think that there is a real human being growing and moving inside me makes me feel good.*

AMBIVALENCE: *Well, I didn't plan this pregnancy and I didn't want it (not quite yet), but I love kids and I sometimes dream of having this baby in my arms.*

ANXIETY: *How can I deal with a husband, with school, and give a baby all the love it needs? I don't think I can do everything. I don't have the money and I know my parents don't have it either.*

FEAR: *I've been sick this whole time and I wonder what it's doing to the baby. Am I hurting my baby? Will it be normal? Will it be deformed or retarded?*

ACCEPTANCE: *I finally had to accept that this was my lot. I had sex, I got pregnant and I had to face the birth of a baby I hadn't really planned or wanted.*

SECOND TRIMESTER

During the second three months, something very special took place in our pregnancies. We began to feel the first movements of life and motherhood took on new meaning. Much of the sickness seemed to have disappeared. Most of us began to experience less fatigue and could begin to face life and school with new energy.

It was also the time we were forced to think seriously about our decisions to keep our babies.

It thrilled me to feel my baby moving within me. At first I couldn't believe it. It felt like butterfly wings.

After a while my nausea and fatigue were over. I felt more energy and felt better about everything.

Once I had decided to keep my baby I could move on with my plans. My mom helped me to begin thinking about the future. Even school got easier.

My husband was so excited we bought a book and started to pick out names that we wanted to give to our baby. He even began to work on a cradle.

I decided to give my baby away because I could never support it. Finally, I had to think about my future without a baby.

Although my parents were great to me I began to resent them. Just when I thought I was getting more freedom, I was more dependent on them than ever. After all, they were paying for things.

My husband was happy about the baby, but I know it was a big change for him, too. He wanted to go out more with his friends. This baby was already taking away his freedom.

THIRD TRIMESTER

As teen mothers getting ready for birth we had concerns about birth. We also faced school, homework and changes in our social life. Those of us who were married had cooking, cleaning and taking care of a husband. Many of us felt overwhelmed when we were faced with all of these responsibilities. During this time it was common to fear everything we had heard about the pain of labor and delivery. Some of us even worried about dying. It was common to be concerned about our babies: Would they be normal? Would they be retarded? Would they die at birth? Those of us in childbirth classes dealt with many of these fears and felt more sure of ourselves.

I think the worst thing is the way you change and look. I used to cry every day. My husband couldn't understand. I would start to get dinner and I would start crying. Anything he would say would start me crying. He would be watching TV and I would be in the bathroom combing my hair and I would cry. It was terrible.

You're always taking everything out on the same person, your husband, or your mom, or somebody in your family.

They get all your anger and your disappointment. One minute you're real happy and the next minute you're just crying your eyes out. You don't even know why.

My third trimester was the hardest because I was so tired all the time. It was hard to keep up with school, the house, and my marriage. I couldn't wait for the baby to be born.

I began to be worried about labor. All my friends had told me how hard it was and I wondered how I was going to handle it.

I was worried about my baby. Would it be all right? Would it be normal? I don't think I could handle a retarded child. I dreamed about labor and birth. I dreamed that my baby was born dead and I screamed. I have a lot of nightmares.

I was excited about birth, especially after I went to Lamaze classes. My husband went with me and we practiced every night. I really looked forward to birth.

My doctor told me that I had toxemia and that I had to stay in bed the last three weeks. My hands and feet swelled up something terrible and I was tired all the time.

Maria: *A lot of us think, "Oh, we're never going to be the way we were before." You look at your old clothes and you wonder, "Will I ever fit into those again?" Last night I went through all of my drawers and I looked at my tiny jeans. I'll never wear them again.*

Kimberly: *I lost all my weight, all of it, every single pound. But I still feel different because I am 16 and I have stretch marks. I think about those and I think, "I can't wear this, or I can't wear that, because they will show."*

SOCIAL CHANGES

Teenage is a time of making friends, dating, partying, and answering questions like "Who am I?" Pregnancy changes your chances for making friends and having the social life you would have as a single person.

BODY IMAGE

Tammy: *I feel fat. I feel like I'm unattractive and I worry about Ricky going out on me because I'm so ugly. I get myself all worked up. There's nothing really to worry about. And then sometimes I feel really great—"Wow, look at me."*

Rachel: *I used to feel fat even before I was pregnant. But everybody said I wasn't. Now I really feel fat and I look it. It's not too good.*

Nancy: *I felt really fat. I didn't feel ugly but I felt fat. But I was also really proud that I was pregnant. And I knew I'd get over the part about being fat. And I did.*

Pregnancy makes you grow up faster. You learn about yourself and your values and you discover the real friends who will support and help you during this time. It helps you realize that the person you choose for a husband must be the man that you want to be the father of your child.

FRIENDS AND FRIENDSHIPS

Tammy: *One of the things that hurt most during pregnancy was that our groups turned up their noses at us. We were no longer part of all the fun things we had done together.*

Holly: *Before we got pregnant it was important that we "fit in." We would do anything to be part of the group. Now most of us are treated like outcasts.*

Christina: *It was the desire to be accepted by my group that pushed me into sex. I didn't really want to do it, but they all put a lot of pressure on me. Now look at me.*

Maria: *I know now it's most important to be yourself. In the long run, you are going to be responsible for making your own choices.*

Nancy: *I go out once in a while, but I'm wary because a lot of guys think, "Wow, she's got a kid! Easy city." But I'm not that way at all and it really turns me off. I don't go out that often.*

Christina: *I'm not living with my family. I'm living with a friend. It's really bleak and confusing. I miss everything I left behind.*

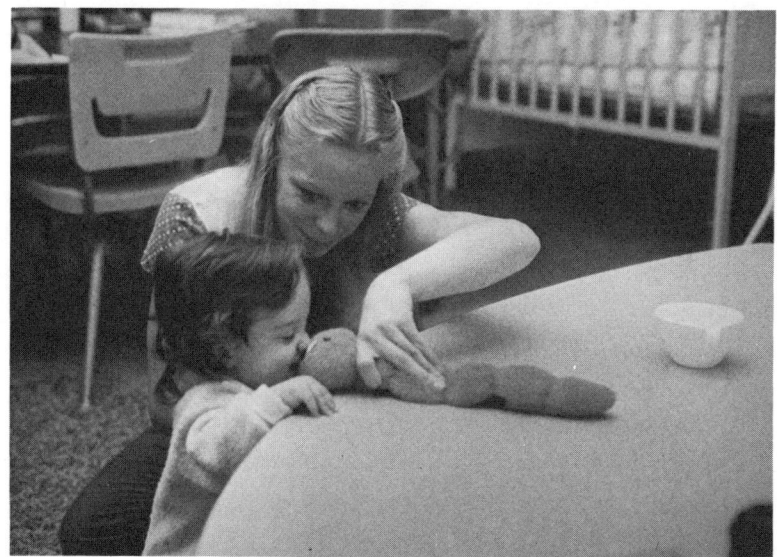

Rachel: *My sister and her friends talk about guys. I can't get into it anymore. I don't know what to do about it. Sometimes I feel depressed.*

Holly: *I don't have any more old friends since I've become pregnant. The type of friends I had don't want to see you when you get pregnant. I realized that if they can't accept me and my baby I had better find other kinds of friends.*

Angela: *When I'm talking to my sister and her friends I feel separated because I've gone through an experience that they haven't. There's nothing else like it and you can't compare it to anything. I can't get into what they're saying because it's school stuff. We go to school here but it's different because we think and learn about babies.*

Kimberly: *My social life has changed drastically. In fact, I don't have one any more. When you have a husband and try to keep a house and try to go to school, you can't keep in contact with all your friends. Even though they keep calling, it's hard.*

Robyn: *There have been a lot of changes. I don't see my friends any more and we're not on the same plane anyway. They say, "We went to this party Saturday night," and I say, "I've been to a doctor's appointment."*

Tina: *My life has changed a lot. When I married I moved out from my family, gave up my career, and left school. I don't have a social life any more. When you have a husband and are trying to keep a house and go to school, you can't keep in contact with your friends.*

Tammy: *I had to give it all up. And it's for the next eighteen years. I think I'll still be young enough to have a social life after my baby's grown up, if I really want it.*

Holly: *This pregnancy has really made me grow up. Now I don't have to be part of the group (I can't anyway because they don't want me.). I realized that the kids I thought were really super cool or who act really smart and leave other people out are really unsure of themselves.*

Tina: *Our best friends have stuck with us. The ones worth having are the friends who will stick with you no matter what. They are the ones who you can have a big fight with and still be friends. You can talk to them no matter what and they understand what you are trying to say. Those are the kind of friends we are going to look for now—not the other kind. The others aren't worth it.*

DATING

Maria: *What guys are going to want us now? It's going to be pretty tough to get a guy to ask you out when you have to tell him that you have to go home in three hours to breastfeed your baby.*

Nancy: *I've learned one thing—I'm not going to date just anybody. I've learned that I'm a valuable human being and that the guys will have to meet certain expectations. I don't want to go to bed on the first date. I want something else from a relationship.*

Rachel: *I go out with just my friends and my sisters. And that's it. I still look at guys and I think, "Oh, if I wasn't pregnant, I'd be chasing them." But all I can do now is look. I'm afraid of how they look at me since I'm pregnant.*

Rebecca: *The father of my baby doesn't want to have a thing to do with me. My friends tell me that I can still go out, but I don't feel like it. When I went out on a date once I didn't even want the guy to come near me. I felt just like crawling in a corner.*

Robyn: *I know that there is going to be someone who will accept me and my baby. I just have to wait and find out who it is. I know that I probably will get married someday. But right now, guys make me really mad.*

RELATIONSHIPS WITH OUR PARENTS

One thing is for sure: pregnancy changed our relationships with our mothers and our fathers. Some of us had good experiences and the full support of our families and some of us didn't.

Maria: *I want to move out soon. It's a hassle because my parents don't want me to do it, because I'm not old enough, or I'm not smart enough, or I can't handle it. My dad doesn't want me to take my baby. But she's mine. I love my mom and dad, and I want them to be close to the baby, but I don't want them to use her against me.*

Cheryl: *This pregnancy and birth has brought our family closer together. I sure appreciate my mother and all the things she did for me when I was a baby. My relationship with my family is just like a marriage—it takes a lot of work and communication.*

Rachel: *My mom and dad sometimes find it hard to accept that I have this responsibility. They went out of town one time and I told my father that I wasn't going. He said, "What? You can't stay here by yourself with the baby." I mean, I'm her mother, I should be able to. I don't get mad at them for it, but sometimes it's really hard to face.*

Robyn: *I'm glad I have my mom. Sometimes I don't want to be independent and sometimes I get so depressed that I think, "Oh, God, I need my mom."*

Kimberly: *My mom and I have a very good relationship. But sometimes she still thinks I'm a little girl. It's hard for her to accept that I have a baby and that I have my own life now and that I'm not at home with her and my dad. It's hard to separate from a good relationship like that.*

Angela: *There are times when my parents overshadow my decisions, and that makes me madder than anything else. The baby is my child and I want to raise her. When I feel that they're doing something wrong, it's hard to say "Don't do that," because they're my parents. I want to feel like I'm strong enough to take care of my baby and I want to prove that to myself, if nobody else.*

Maria: *I know that it's going to be hard to leave home. And it's kind of scary. But I think it's harder for me staying at home. Sometimes my mom says, "Let the baby cry. There is nothing wrong with that." So I let the baby cry for a few minutes and my sister comes charging in, "What's the matter with you? Take care of your kid. She's screaming." Then everybody starts at everybody else, and I always get the worst end of it because it's my baby.*

Holly: *If I thought I didn't have freedom before the baby I didn't know what freedom was. My parents watch every step I take. After all, they are paying for me and my baby.*

SUPPORT

The most important thing you can do is to get yourself a support system that can help you through your pregnancy. It might include your husband, your boyfriend, your parents, your friends, your teachers, or your counselors. No one has all these people for support, but the more people you have, the better you can cope with the mixed feelings of your pregnancy.

HOW CAN I GET A SUPPORT SYSTEM?

Your job is to find yourself a support system that you can count on. Part of your support system is based on luck. (That is, you are lucky if you have a supportive husband, boyfriend, or parents.) The other part is based on surrounding yourself only with the kind of people that you can trust. The first step in doing this is to be the kind of person that others can trust so that you, in turn, attract that kind of person. The second step is getting rid of those "friends" and acquaintances that you cannot count on. The third step is to ask for and accept help when you need it.

WHERE DO I LOOK FOR A SUPPORT SYSTEM?

Look around you. First, look to your partner, your family and your friends. Look to your community for classes, institutions, organizations and professionals that can give you information, support and confidence when you need it.

WHAT IF I DON'T HAVE A HUSBAND (PARENTS, FRIENDS, ETC.)?

There is no one right support system. No one person has a totally complete support system. Some people have strong marriages but no parents to support them. Others have no husbands or boyfriends but strong parent support. Some have just friends to help them. Others need strength within themselves to make up for the shortcomings in their support systems.

YOURSELF

The first place to look for support is within yourself. What are the strengths that you have that will help you through this experience? Patience, gentleness, kindness, a sense of humor and an ability to put things in perspective are all valuable qualities.

Angela: *It's been hard. But the one thing I've learned is that you've got to be strong.*

I know that in the end I can count on myself and my strength.

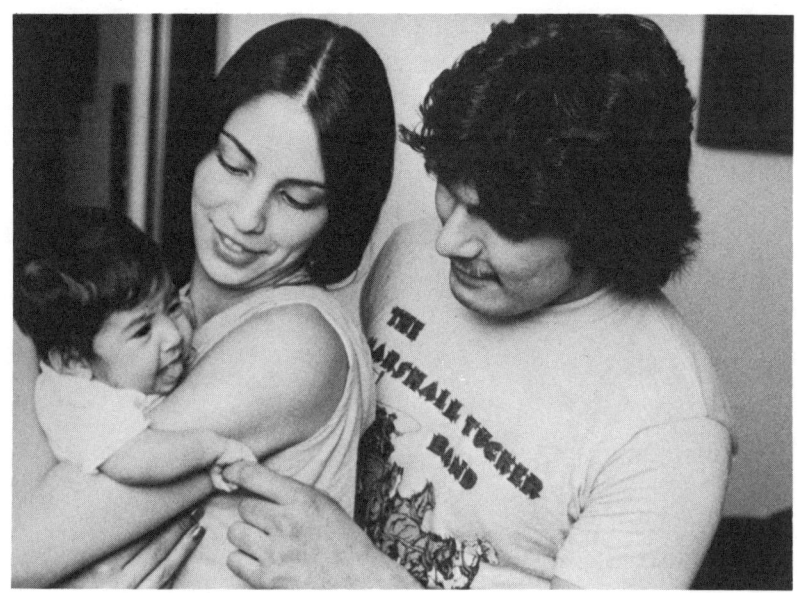

PARTNER

The next place to look for support is in your husband or boyfriend. The qualities to look for are strength, trust, compassion, caring, and concern. If he is not supportive, look to another person with whom you have established trust, such as your mother, sister, or friend.

> Kimberly: *The good thing about being married is that my husband is always there to take care of the baby when I need it. He gives me support and he gives the baby support.*

FAMILY

When you become pregnant, not only are you a mother, but your parents are grandparents and your brothers and sisters are uncles and aunts. No one in your family is untouched by the birth of your baby. Many times you and your mother become closer than you have ever been. It may take time for your father to get used to the idea, but many fathers become the best support, financially, physically and emotionally.

> Maria: *I always get positive reinforcement from my mom. My mom is always there. When I say, "Oh, Mom, I'm so scared," she says, "What's wrong, honey?" For a while I had a pain and I was scared. She said, "Don't be scared—it's normal." Sisters can give you support too.*

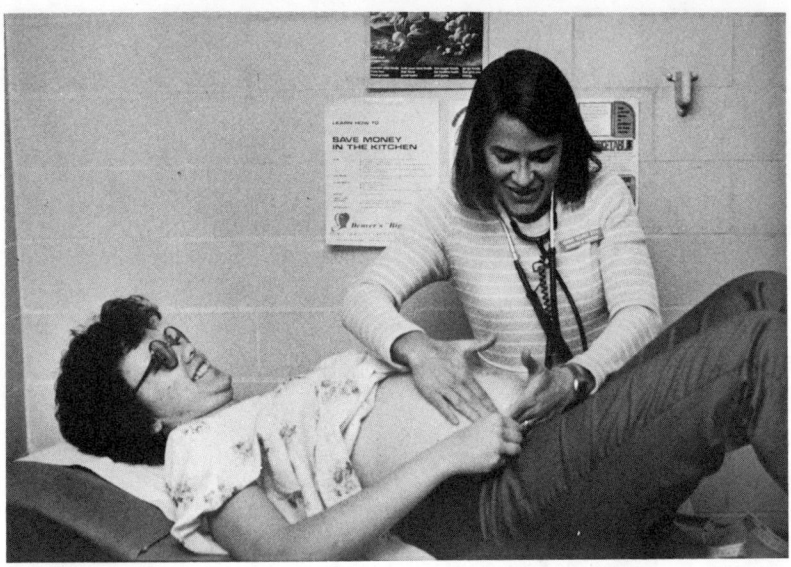

FRIENDS

Those of you who do not have the support of the fathers of your babies or the support of your parents may find you can turn to a friend or friends for the support you need. It is especially helpful if you have a friend who has been pregnant and can give you special information and support.

> Theresa: *Some friends get really close to you and they want to help. One of my friends, after I had Sandy, came over every day, changed his diapers and the whole bit. I thought it was terrific! Because she has her own nephews, she knows all about that stuff.*

PROFESSIONALS

Perhaps you have a personal physician or a nurse in your prenatal clinic who can give you the support you need. It's important that you ask them for help. Remember there is no such thing as a stupid question. Make lists of questions and take them with you on your visits. Should you need spiritual help, turn to your minister, rabbi or priest. It is their job to help you.

> Molly: *I go to a doctor who never tells me anything. But the nurse is so nice. She's a woman and knows what pregnancy is and how I feel. The doctor is a man and men will never know how women feel during pregnancy. At least the nurse knows I'm not just complaining and that it really does hurt. If I go to the clinic with a problem, that nurse is the one place I can get support.*

SCHOOL

A school for teen moms gives you the opportunity to share your concerns and needs with others who are or have been in the same situation. Also look to teachers who are especially sympathetic. Or, perhaps you can turn to a counselor, someone who has the skills and knowledge to help you.

Maria: *This teen moms' program is great. My mom's had kids, but she doesn't quite remember how it was, staying up at three o'clock in the morning. You can't say, "I've got to get away from my child," because people will think you're an awful mother. We have support and understanding here at school. Teen mothers understand where you're coming from and how hard it is to take care of your child all the time.*

COMMUNITY

Each community has its own set of resources. Look into childbirth classes, prenatal and parenting classes. Check out adult education centers, Red Cross, Planned Parenthood, Choices, March of Dimes, the YMCA and YWCA. Don't hesitate to ask for the information and support you need.

Robyn: *The best thing that ever happened to me was Lamaze classes. I learned all about me and my baby. It was great because there were other girls there just like me.*

SUPPORT SYSTEM

Who are you going to turn to in times of need? Put the names and telephone numbers of those persons you can trust. Remember, no one can really expect a 100% support system.

YOURSELF

List qualities you can turn to when you need them.

1. _____
2. _____
3. _____

HUSBAND/BOYFRIEND/PARTNER

List qualities you can turn to when you need them.

1. _____
2. _____
3. _____

FAMILY

List family members and telephone numbers:

Mother _____

Father _____

Sisters/brothers _____

Aunts/uncles _____

Grandparents _____

FRIENDS

List those friends you can turn to when you need help physically, financially, emotionally, or spiritually.

1. _____
2. _____
3. _____

SCHOOL

Teacher _____

Counselor _____

Teen Moms' class _____

Vo Tech _____

Adult Education _____

PROFESSIONALS

Doctor _____

Midwife _____

Nurse _____

Childbirth teacher _____

Clinic _____

Minister, rabbi, priest _____

Other _____

COMMUNITY

Red Cross _____

Planned Parenthood _____

Choices _____

YWCA _____

March of Dimes _____

Other _____

ADVICE

Another kind of support is advice. Teen moms are given all kinds of advice. Some is good and some is bad.

Nancy: *I had this habit of overdressing my baby. My sister would walk in and say, "Oh, my God, what is wrong with this kid? You are going to make her sweat to death and then she's going to get a cold." Who's the mother here and who makes the decisions?*

Maria: *My aunts tell me not to spoil my kid. But I want to mother my own child. They sit there and say, "Don't do this, don't do that," and I just want to give up. They tell all the old wives tales. When I was pregnant, my aunt said, "Don't look at the full moon when you are pregnant." I asked, "Why not?" And she said, "Because your baby will get a big brown mark on its face." I asked my mother, "Is that true?" She said, "None of my babies were marked and I've seen the moon before."*

Holly: *If I think I'm given good advice, I'll take it. If I don't agree, then I say forget it. I appreciate it as long as it's not forced down my throat.*

Tina: *It depends on how you're told. If someone says, "Give me that baby. You are not doing that right," that would make me mad. But it's different if someone says, "Well, I tried it this way and it worked for me and it might work for you." It depends on how it's said.*

Rebecca: *I've decided that I'll take and think about any advice. I appreciate people caring about me. But, if I don't agree, and I start doing it differently and they keep harassing me, I'm going to say, "Hey, I think it's better this way. Read this book I was reading and maybe that will change your mind."*

Kimberly: *The strongest advice giver is your own mother because it's her grandchild and she's been telling you what to do since you were born. I was always worried about what my mother was going to say. But, she pretty much has let me make my own decisions. I tell her the decisions I have made and then she tells me what she thinks about it. Last night I told her about my decision to breastfeed and she said, "I am so glad you are going to do that. I think it's best but I don't want to tell you what to do." So, I'm not worried about her telling me how to raise my baby.*

Nancy: *My mom really helped me. I live next door to my mom and she let me do everything myself unless I asked her for help. When she could see that I was ready to pull out my hair, she came next door and helped me. But, she encouraged me to do everything myself. And if I had a question, I could call her up and she was more than willing to help me. But, she won't say, "Nancy, do this."*

Theresa: *My mother-in-law thinks everything I do is wrong and everything's got to be done her way. I was giving the baby a bath and I was washing his hair and she said, "Don't wash his hair that way. Wash it this way." I said, "You know, I think I'm doing a pretty good job. I'd rather do it the way I've been doing it." If I buy the baby something, she'll say, "Oh, that's not good enough." Then she'll go out and buy him practically the same thing but just made by a different person. She drives me up the wall!*

How Can I Be Pregnant And Stay In School?

CHALLENGE:

Pregnancy is the single greatest cause of school dropout among female students in the United States. If you drop out of school, you will probably never complete a high school education and you are more likely to join the ranks of mothers who have a hard time finding jobs.

CHOICE:

If you are a teen mom who chooses to complete high school you are far more likely to get a good job and far less likely to require public financial assistance.

QUOTE:

"No matter how you look at it, and no matter what situation— married, single, or whatever—it's money that's really the most important thing. If you don't have money, there's not going to be happiness."

QUESTIONS:

Why is it important that I finish school?
What choices do I have?
What is a teen mom program?
How can I stay in high school?
Why should I get vocational training?
How can I find out about vocational programs?
What if I haven't finished high school?
What kind of programs can I get at vocational schools?

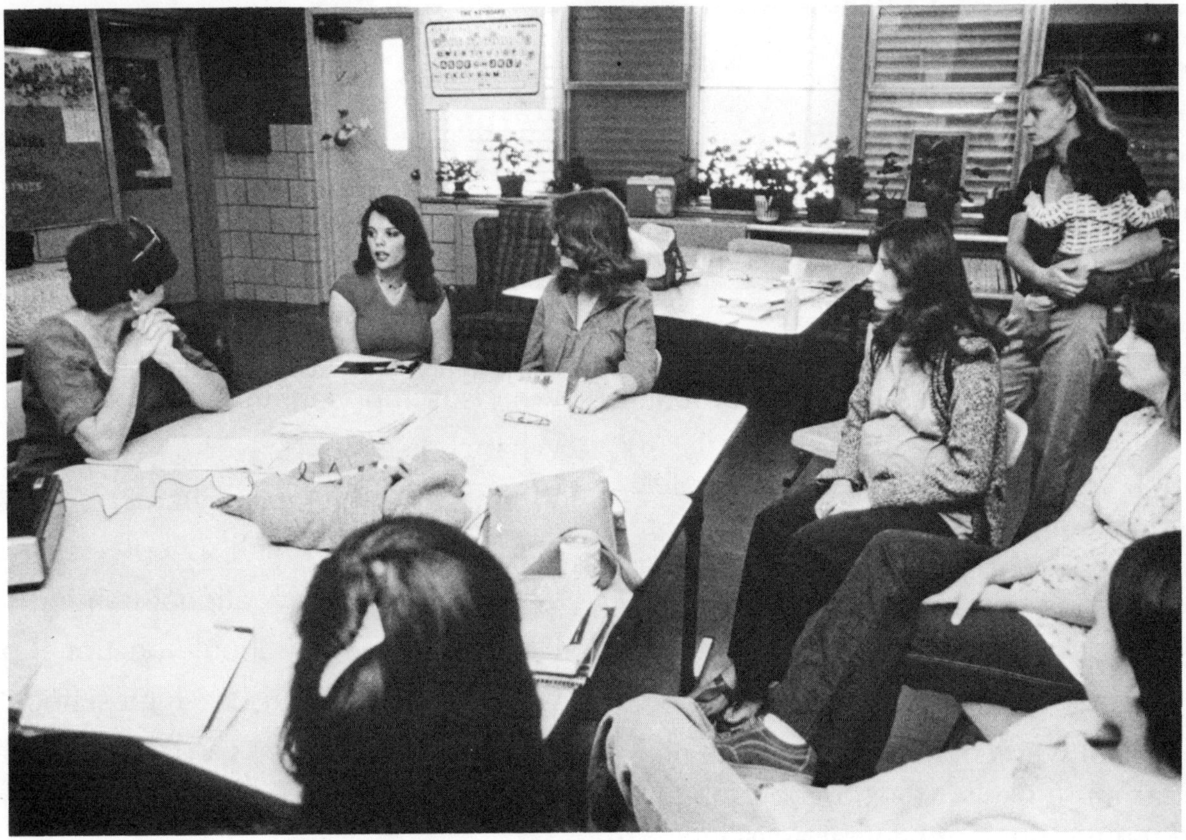

EGG

SCHOOLING
KENTUCKY FRIED
HIGH

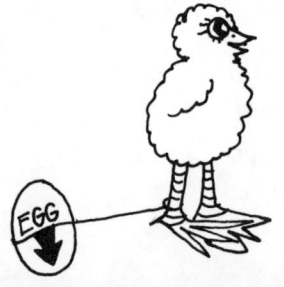

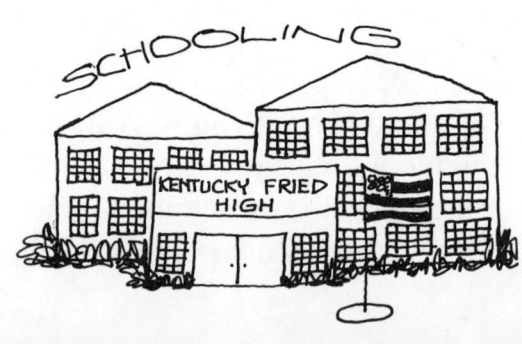

WHY IS IT IMPORTANT THAT I FINISH HIGH SCHOOL?

We have to prepare for our futures and we also have to give our babies the best possible start in life. Being pregnant and being in school is really hard. When we found out we were pregnant we all thought about dropping out of school. We all have friends and sisters who, when they found they were pregnant, dropped out. However, we know how hard it is for them to get any kind of a job. Most of them had to turn to welfare. And we didn't want to do that. Once they got on welfare, they had a terrible time getting off it. Some of them never did—and never will.

When you are pregnant and going to keep your baby, you know that you have not only your own life and own future to consider but your baby's as well.

WHY IS EDUCATION IMPORTANT?

All of us are going to have to be able to support ourselves some time. Those of us who are going to keep our babies are going to have to support them too.

Education is not just a luxury—it's a necessity. What kind of jobs can we expect to get if we don't have high school diplomas or some kind of job training? It's also important that, as mothers, we are able to read and understand instructions for our babies, for instance reading medicine labels. We're going to need math for buying food. We're going to have to know something about the world.

WHAT KIND OF CHOICES DO WE HAVE?

First, you can stay in your regular school where at least you can get the credits you need to graduate. But, that's pretty hard and none of us could do it. It's hard to face your old friends and teachers. It's also hard to be pregnant (going to the bathroom all the time) and go to regular school.

Second, you can attend night school or adult education courses. This is a little better because you aren't facing your friends. But, it's hard to be around all those adults when you don't have much in common with them.

Third, there is sometimes home tutoring if you are too sick to go to school. But again, that isn't much fun and you don't see anybody.

Alternative Teen Program

In our community, there is a special teen parenting program for girls like us. You can go there when you are pregnant and stay there through the birth of your baby. When your baby is born, if you decide to keep it, you can continue school and just bring your baby along. There is a special nursery and a lady to take care of the baby while you are in school.

Our teen program (there are over 400 in the United States) allows you to:

1. Stay in school.
2. Get a support system to meet your special needs.
3. Get skills in prenatal care, childbirth and postnatal care.
4. Get skills in family living, parenting, health, nutrition, clothing and consumerism.
5. Prepare for work in clerical, secretarial and business positions.
6. Explore careers and job search skills.
7. Continue your classes in science, math, English and social studies.

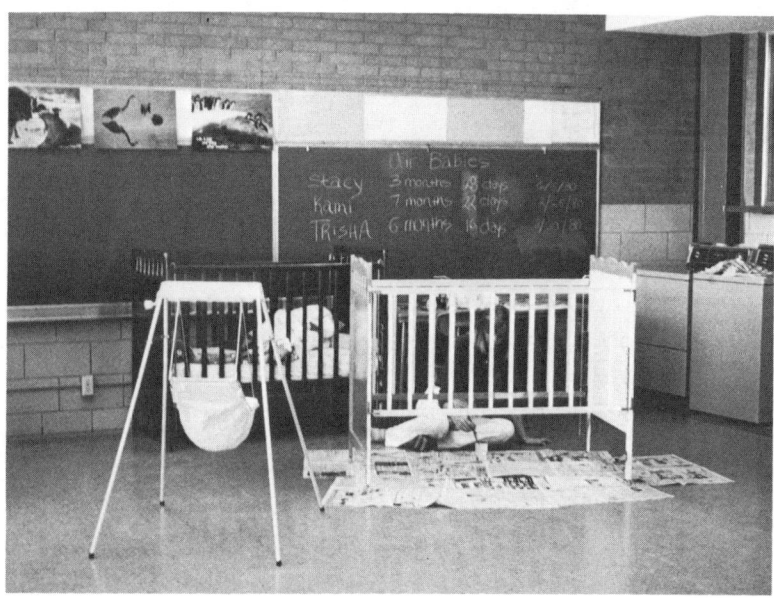

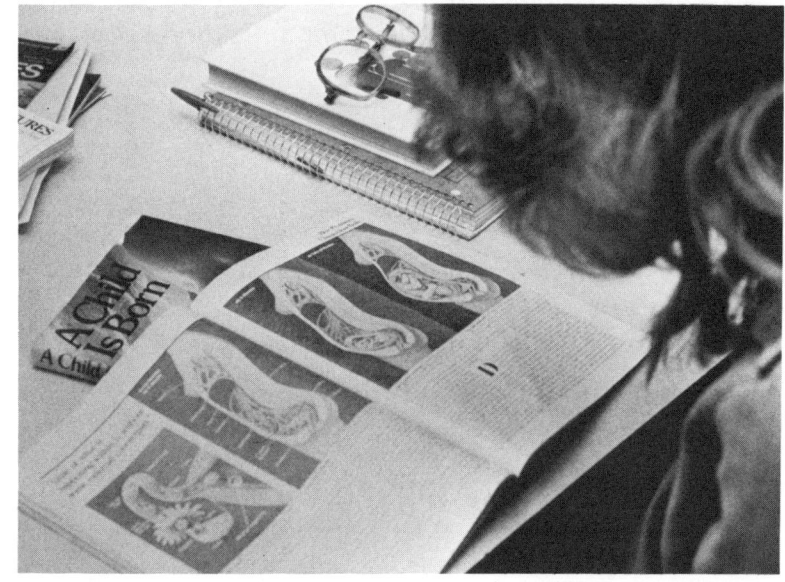

WHAT HAS THIS TEEN PREGNANCY PROGRAM GIVEN YOU?

Maria: *It was my last alternative. I think I would have dropped out of school. I couldn't leave my baby at a day care center. I feel that if it hadn't been for this teen mom's program I would have been staying home everyday and I wouldn't have learned as much.*

Tina: *I went back to regular school and I worked until six o'clock. My baby stayed with the babysitter all day. I missed her so much. After the third week, I told my mom to forget it. I was just going to stay home. My mom read about this teen moms' program in the paper and here I am and I am going to graduate!*

Kimberly: *I felt that the program helped me develop skills to be a better mother and a better wife. We learned things like child development and communication skills.*

Robyn: *The best thing that happened to me is that I learned office skills. I learned data entry and I already have a job for next year.*

Angela: *The teachers were really interested in us. They understood what we were going through and how important our babies were.*

Cheryl: *The best part was the way the students got along together. We were able to answer questions and give suppsort to each other. Everyone understood how hard it is to be young and have a baby at the same time.*

Christina: *The nursery was a happy place for our babies and for us. We learned parenting skills from the woman who took care of our babies.*

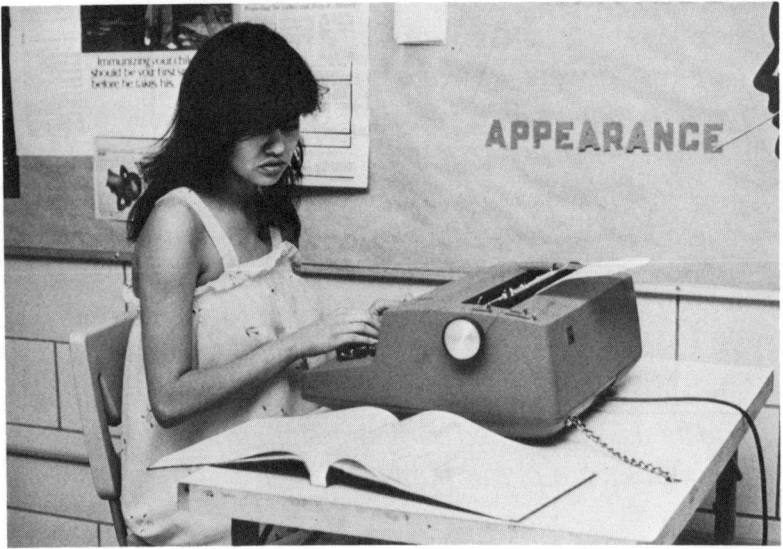

WHY SHOULD I GET VOCATIONAL TRAINING?

Pregnant teens who have not finished school are the most likely to be unemployed and the most likely to begin the cycle of poverty that will not be broken for the rest of their lives. When you have a high school degree (or the equivalent) and some kind of vocational skills, you will be able to find better paying jobs and can avoid the welfare trap.

WHAT DO YOU WANT FOR YOUR FUTURE?

Look at the ads in the Help Wanted section of your local newspaper. Look them over carefully and answer these questions:

What job would you like to choose for your future?

Which are the jobs that are most interesting for you?

Which jobs can you see yourself in this year?

Which jobs can you see yourself doing in five years?

Which are the jobs that have the most attractive setting?

Which are the jobs that you could get without a high school diploma?

Which are the jobs that you could get right now?

Which are the jobs that you could get if you signed up for any of the vocational training classes listed on the following page.

HOW CAN I FIND OUT ABOUT VOCATIONAL PROGRAMS?

To find out about vocational programs, you can contact a school guidance counselor, a social worker or a rehabilitation counselor in the state employment office. These people will be able to give you information and assistance concerning programs that could be available to you. Some welfare agencies can give you the information you need.

WHAT IF I HAVEN'T FINISHED HIGH SCHOOL?

If you do not finish high school, you can take a high school general equivalency diploma (G.E.D.) The test covers your knowledge of English, math, history and science without making you take the courses. If you are enrolled in a vocational program you can take the G.E.D. at the same time.

WHAT KIND OF PROGRAMS CAN I GET AT VOCATIONAL SCHOOLS?

Each school in each area differs in content. But all programs are designed to prepare you for entry level employment and advancement opportunities within your community.

Listed here are careers that you may prepare for at a vocational/technical school. Look carefully at the list. Where would you like to see yourself?

ACCOUNTING & DATA PROCESSING:
Bank clerks, office clerks, file clerks, bookkeepers and accountants.

EARLY CHILDHOOD EDUCATION:
Managerial positions, operators of self-owned child care center or day care home.

HEALTH OCCUPATIONS:
Aides for laboratory, X-ray technicians, dental assistants, doctors' assistants.

HORTICULTURE—LANDSCAPING:
Landscape designers and workers in nurseries, garden centers, sod farms, parks, golf courses, greenhouses and floral shops.

FLORAL DESIGN:
Flower dealers, nursery attendants and floral designers, interior landscapers.

RADIO & TELEVISION:
Technical assistants in audio-visual for radio, TV, schools and hospitals.

VOCATIONAL AGRICULTURE:
Livestock and crop workers, agriculture mechanics.

COMPUTER OPERATIONS:
Junior computer operators, peripheral operators, input/output control clerks, tape librarians.

BUSINESS PROGRAMMING:
Junior programmers, programmer trainees and maintenance programmers.

BUSINESS MINI-COMPUTER OPERATIONS:
Small business mini-computer operators.

DATA ENTRY OPERATIONS:
Data entry operators.

COSMETOLOGY:
Beauticians, (permanent waving, haircutting, styling, shampooing, tinting, manicures, facial treatments, make-up analysis, wig styling, iron curling, blow drying).

ELECTRONICS TECHNOLOGY:
Electronic technicians, electronic parts clerks and salespeople, electronic sales and services.

NURSE AIDES AND ORDERLIES

OFFICE OCCUPATIONS:
Secretaries, clerical employees, typists, machine transcribers, file clerks, office machine operators and basic accountants.

PRINTING TRADES:
Pressmen, general printers, camera assistants, screen printers, cutter operators, binders or assistant pressmen.

TECHNICAL DRAWING:
Mechanical, civil, or technical drafters.

OUR EXPERIENCES WITH VOCATIONAL/CAREER TRAINING

Holly: *I've got my certificate in data processing and already have a good job at IBM. They are going to train me some more.*

Rachel: *I've got my degree in cosmetology and already have a job at the beauty salon. That way I can move out of my parents' house and get an apartment of my own.*

Maria: *My husband has been accepted at the university and I'm going along with him. With my data processing I know I can get a job anywhere.*

Kimberly: *I have a certificate in child guidance and I am going to try to get a job at the day care center. That way I can take my baby and also earn some money for us.*

Robyn: *I got my training in office skills. I have a job with the church, but next spring I am going to work for social security. My parents have been awfully good to me but I have to get out on my own.*

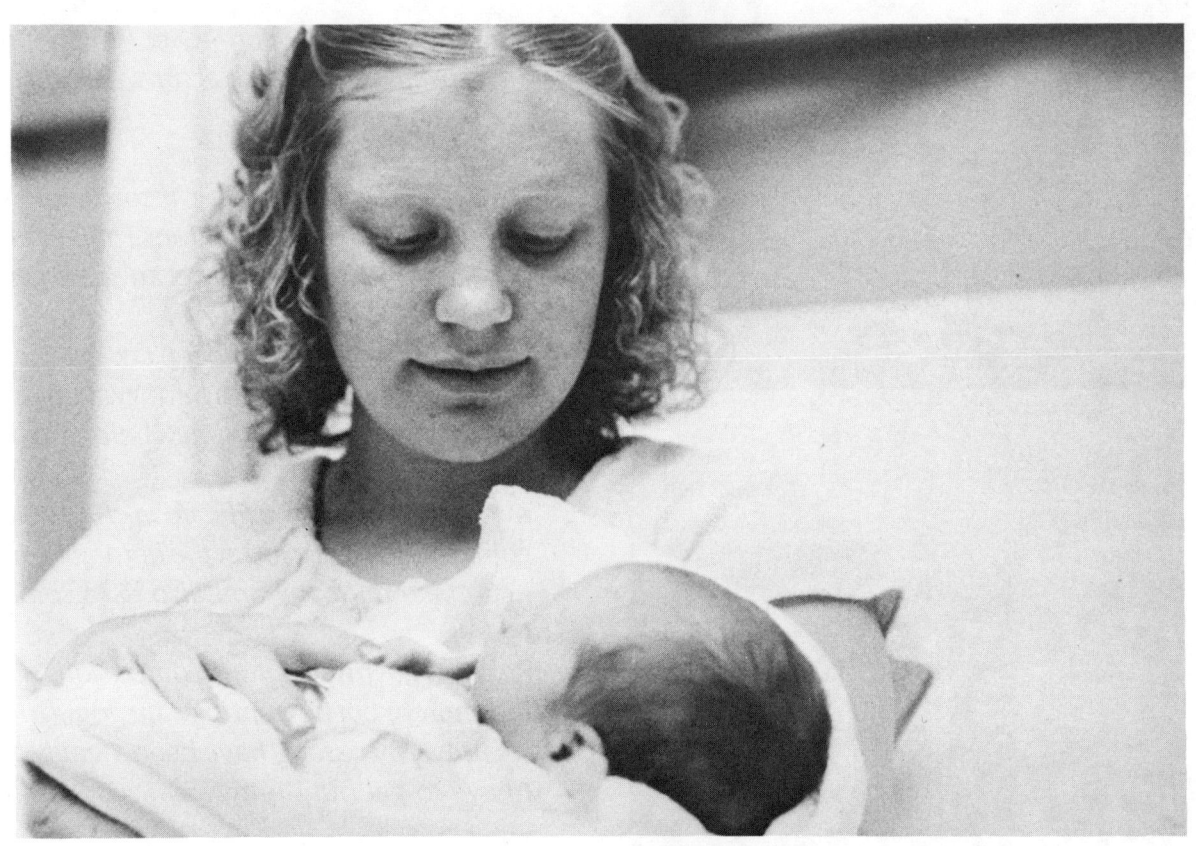

Childbirth: The Greatest Challenge

CHALLENGE:

Childbirth is the greatest challenge you will ever face. The more afraid and tense you are during birth, the longer and harder your labor will be on you and your baby.

CHOICE:

When you choose to join childbirth classes and learn ways to help yourself during childbirth, it is easier on you and your baby.

QUOTE:

"My mom can't explain to me what I need to know about childbirth, and I don't even know what to ask. What I need to know is what is going to happen to me, why it's happening and how I can help myself."

QUESTIONS:

What is labor and why is it called that?
Why is birth supposed to be so painful?
Why should I be awake during labor?
How does the baby get out?
How does the uterus open?
How can relaxation help me?
How is breathing supposed to help in labor?
Does it hurt to push the baby out?
How can my husband/boyfriend/friend help me?
What is a cesarean and why do they do it?
What can go wrong in labor and delivery?
How long does birth last?

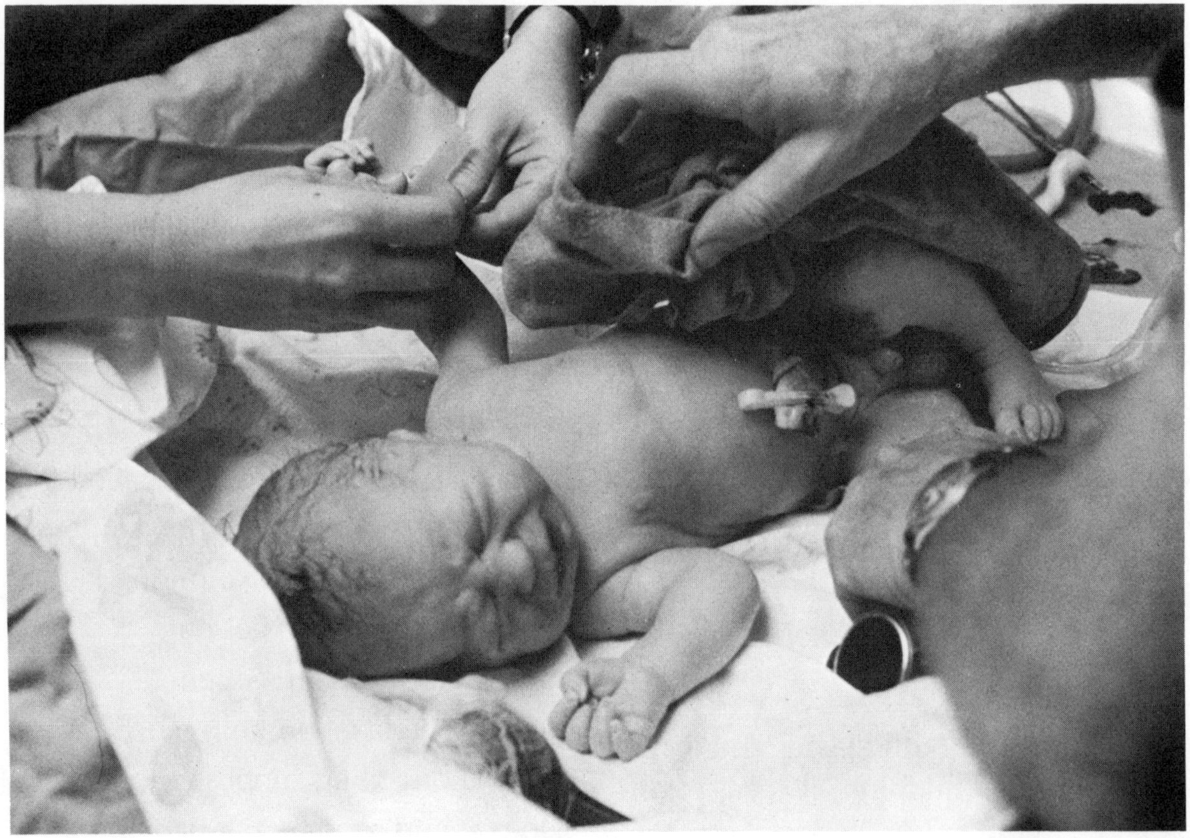

WHAT DOES CHILDBIRTH MEAN TO YOU?

What is the first thing that comes to your mind when you think of birth?

Baby? _____

Pain? _____

Suffering? _____

Blood? _____

Joy? _____

Creation? _____

Work? _____

Boy—Girl? _____

Fear? _____

Excitement? _____

All of these words, and then some, explain what birth is all about.

Birth is a baby.

Birth is a lot of work.

Pain, suffering and blood are associated with childbirth.

Joy and creation are part of one of the most creative acts of a woman's life.

The sex of your baby is important to you and the father.

Fear of the unknown and fear of what is going to happen to you and the baby are important parts of birth.

Lastly, birth includes excitement, the thought of new life, and finally seeing your baby.

WHY IS BIRTH SUPPOSED TO BE PAINFUL?

We have all heard stories of birth as painful, nightmarish and horribly long. If a mother goes into birth without any preparation or skills to help herself, her birth can very easily be such a nightmare.

> Christina: *I didn't know what was going to happen to me. I started to have little pains and went right to the hospital. When I got there they said nothing was going on, but they put me to bed anyway. They gave me something to start labor. The pains got so bad I wanted to cry. They left me alone a lot and it was so awful I screamed. I really believed God was punishing me for getting pregnant. By the time the baby came I was so exhausted I didn't care if I had an elephant. I told them to take the baby away.*

DOES BIRTH HAVE TO BE THAT BAD?

Not all of us had births like that. The mothers who went into birth with an understanding of what was happening to them, special techniques to help them in labor and coaches to help them told stories of a joyful, glorious experience.

> Kimberly: *My labor was different. I went to Lamaze classes. I learned everything that was going to happen to me and what I could do to help myself. Mark learned how to rub my back and stroke my legs. He talked to me all through labor and I don't think I could have done it without him. My contractions sure weren't painless but I was able to work with them. I liked the deep breathing and, although it was hard to relax, Mark helped me with every contraction. When my baby came it was the most wonderful moment of my life. When they laid her in my arms, we both cried at being part of such a wonderful miracle.*

BIRTH CLASSES

WHY DO YOU HAVE TO PREPARE FOR LABOR?

Labor is hard work. The journey for your baby from your uterus to the outside takes from eight to twelve hours and is a long, interesting experience for both of you.

We don't know what kind of a labor or delivery you are going to have. We don't know whether it will be a short, easy, painless labor or a long, hard, painful one. What we do know is that if you are able to relax and if you have a coach who is able to give you encouragement and comfort, you will remember the experience with good feelings.

Preparation for childbirth will give you information on:

- What's going to happen to you.

- Breathing exercises to help you cope with labor.

- Relaxation techniques to make your labor shorter.

- Coaching techniques to make you more comfortable.

WHY SHOULD I BE AWAKE DURING LABOR?

We now know that a mother who is awake during labor and delivery gives her baby a healthier start. Both she and her baby recover more quickly after birth. There are some times, however, when medical intervention or anesthetics are required for the safety and health of the baby and the mother.

WHAT HAPPENS TO YOU IN BIRTH?

Probably the thing that will help you the most during your labor is knowing what is happening. In Chapter 2 you learned how the baby got into your uterus. Now that your baby is ready to come into the world, you will learn how nature designed you and your baby for the childbirth experience.

There are three obstacles your baby must pass:

1. Your uterus.

2. Your pelvis.

3. Your vagina.

HOW DOES MY BABY GET THROUGH THE UTERUS?

Your uterus is not only the shelter for your baby during pregnancy, it is also a great muscle that is able to open up to let your baby out during birth. Do you remember the opening at the bottom of your uterus called the cervix? This is where your baby comes out. The cervix is just like the neck of turtle-neck sweater. Imagine trying to get this sweater over a small child's head. The cervix works exactly the same. As the muscles of the uterus pull (these are called contractions), they tug up on the cervix, first thinning it out, and then opening it up all the way to the size of your baby's head.

HOW DO THE CONTRACTIONS OPEN UP THE UTERUS?

Contractions are the tensing and relaxing of your uterus. A contraction is like a great wave: it starts slowly, builds up to a great peak and lets off—and then there is a rest period. Again it starts up slowly, reaches a peak and lets off. During labor the contractions start off as little waves and you hardly know you are having them. As labor continues they become stronger and stronger and longer and longer until your baby is born.

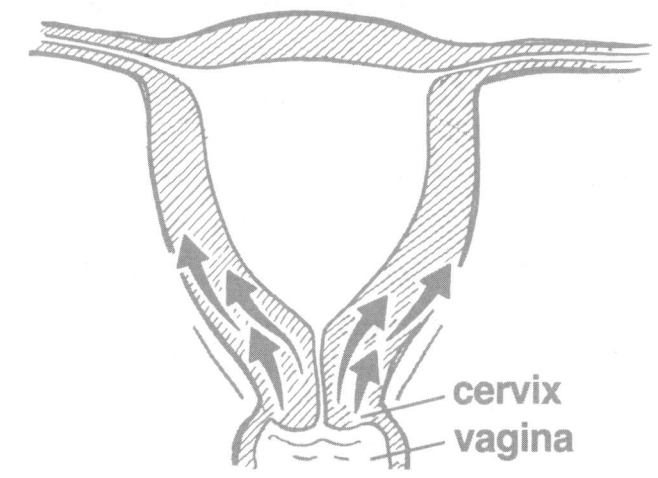

There are three phases of labor before you push your baby's head out:

1. Early—small contractions
2. Active—strong contractions
3. Transition—very strong contractions

When you know what is happening to you it is easier to cope with these contractions.

EARLY LABOR: During the first part of labor, your contractions are thinning out the cervix. Your doctor will call this period EFFACEMENT. These contractions are very mild; they don't last long and you have a lot of time in between contractions. You probably will be at home wondering if you are really in labor.

The contractions last for about 30-60 seconds and you usually become aware of them as they decrease from 20 minutes to 5 minutes apart. You may feel like you have the flu. You may notice an increase in vaginal discharge. Some women describe these contractions like the cramps they have during their periods. Some women have diarrhea and an increased need to urinate.

You may be feeling very excited and yet a little afraid about labor. A lot of women feel relieved that labor is finally here. This phase takes from six to eight hours with your first baby.

ACTIVE LABOR: During the second part of labor, your contractions become stronger and longer. Now their job is to open the cervix to the size of your baby's head. Of course, this takes more muscular effort and your contractions become longer and more intense. The contractions last from 45-60 seconds and are from five to three minutes apart. You know you are in active labor when you experience more pain or discomfort in your back, hips and legs. You may notice an increase in mucous. Toward the end of active labor (as your cervix becomes more opened) you may doubt your ability to cope with labor and won't want to be left alone. This phase takes from 3 to 6 hours for your first baby.

TRANSITION: During the third part of your labor your contractions change. Up until now they have been working at opening your cervix. Toward the end, as your baby moves down in your pelvis, you will feel a great need to push down. These contractions become very long and strong and this may be the most difficult part of your labor. The transition may take from 20 minutes to one hour and this is the time you have to work the hardest. These contractions are extremely

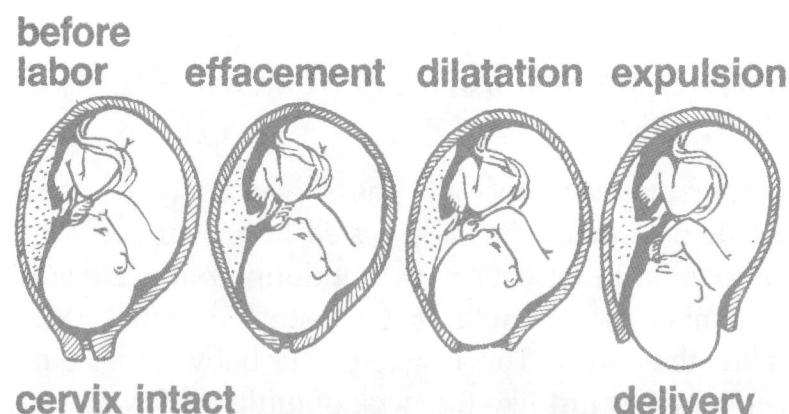

before labor / cervix intact — effacement — dilatation — expulsion / delivery

strong, lasting 60-90 seconds and you may have only one minute in between. Along with the overwhelming desire to push you will feel pressure on your pelvic floor and your rectum. You may even have the desire to sleep and escape. Many women feel a loss of control; they get restless and irritable, maybe even panicky and discouraged. This is the time you will need the most support.

EXPULSION: Finally, after the cervix has been completely thinned out and opened to the size of your baby's head, you will be ready to push your baby through the birth canal. The contractions become less intense. They last about 60 seconds and you will once again have rest intervals of 1-3 minutes in between. You probably will feel a lot of pressure in your rectum and on your pelvic floor. During the expulsion phase, many mothers experience a surgical incision widening the opening to the vagina. This procedure, called an episiotomy, is designed to allow a baby to be delivered without tearing the vaginal tissues. It usually feels good to push and women feel excitement and exhilaration during the expulsion. If you were sleepy before, now you are wide awake and your energy returns.

PLACENTA DELIVERY: After your baby is pushed out, your contractions do not stop. The moment your baby is born, the sudden shrinking of your uterus detaches the placenta (or afterbirth) from the uterine wall. Within the next several minutes, the contractions cause your placenta to become completely detached and the contractions push the placenta through your vagina. The umbilical cord, which attaches your baby to the placenta, is cut midway between the placenta and the baby. If you had an episiotomy, it is repaired with stitches.

POSTPARTUM: This is the time your baby is first laid into your arms. During this time the beautiful emotional attachment between you and your baby takes place. Yours is the first face and the first voice that your baby hears. Your baby falls in love with you and you with your baby. Even if you have chosen to give your baby up for adoption, this is an important part of letting your baby go.

PROGRESSIVE RELAXATION
(HOW TO RELAX YOUR BODY WHILE
YOUR UTERUS IS CONTRACTING)

During labor the one thing your body wants to do most is tense up. Since your uterus is tensing, the rest of your body naturally wants to follow. Unfortunately, when you tense up, you cause your labor to be longer, you feel more pain, your baby gets less oxygen and you are more tired.

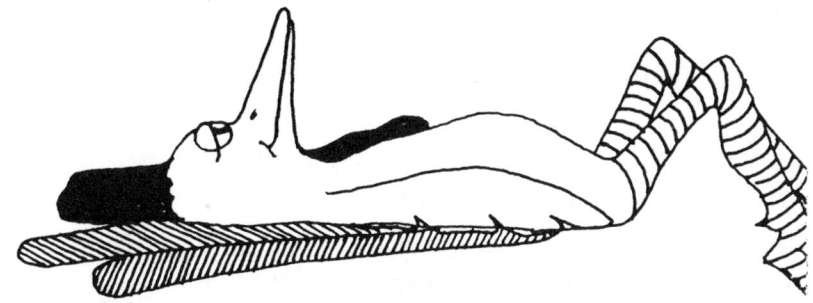

Knowing how to relax during labor will help you to:

- Remain calm.
- Feel less pain.
- Be more energetic.
- Shorten your labor.

RELAXATION: The exercises you learn will help you to relax your feet, legs, thighs, buttocks, hands, shoulders, throat and face during labor—all while your uterus is contracting. Of course, you will have to be in good condition, so you must practice now (much like an athlete must practice for the Olympics).

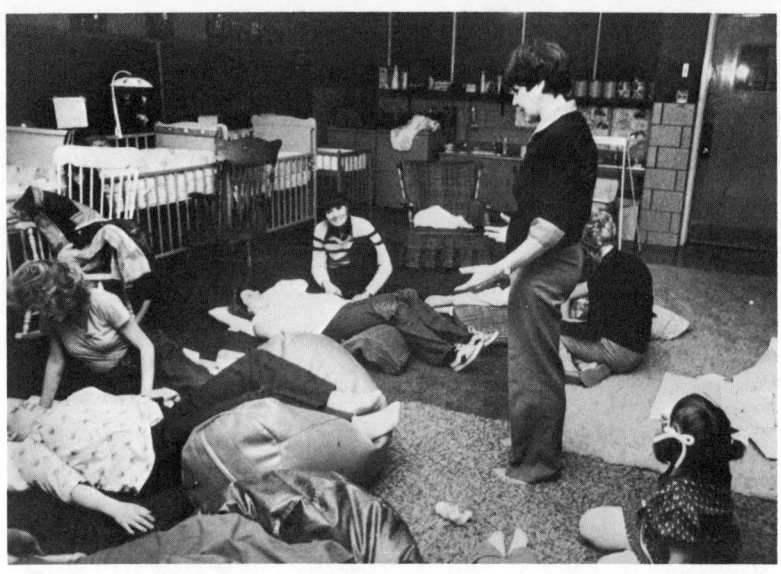

POSITION, BREATHING AND VISUALIZATION

You can use relaxation techniques during pregnancy, during labor and during delivery—and for the rest of your life in times of stress. There are three major things—position, breathing and visualization—that will make your relaxing even better.

POSITION

There are three positions you can use when you do your relaxation exercises.

Back position: Lie on your back with pillows under your head and knees. (This tilts your pelvis.) Let your arms rest naturally and comfortably at your sides and let your legs flop open at the thighs.

Side-lying position: Lie on your side with a pillow under your head. Bend your upper knee (to tilt your pelvis) and put a pillow under it (to keep the blood from being cut off in your legs). Let your bottom leg rest naturally. Rest your arms where they are comfortable.

Sitting position: Sit in a comfortable chair where your back and arms are supported. Let your arms rest comfortably.

BREATHING

When you are in a nice comfortable position, begin to concentrate on your breathing patterns. Find a slow, easy, natural breathing pattern. As you breathe in, breathe in warm relaxing air through your nose. Feel it spread relaxation throughout your body. As you breathe out through your lips, concentrate on letting all the tension out of your body.

VISUALIZATION

Another aid you might find helpful for relaxing your body is visualizing (that is imagining) such feelings as:

Limp as a rag doll

Limp as a piece of spaghetti

Floating like a leaf on the ocean

Light as a feather

Warm and heavy

Melting like butter

Find the words that are helpful to you in your relaxation.

COMPLETE RELAXATION

To learn how to relax during labor, you must first be able to relax each part of your body from your head to your toes.

Practice complete relaxation: Tense up your entire body. Now relax it. Breathe in five deep breaths and with each breath get yourself even more relaxed. Concentrate on how good it feels to be relaxed and how painful it is to be tense.

Practice tensing and relaxing each part of your body:

Tense your feet—relax them.

Tense your calves—relax them.

Tense your thighs—relax them.

Tense your buttocks—relax them.

Tense your stomach muscles—relax them.

Tense your chest—relax it.

Tense your shoulders—relax them.

Tense your arms—relax them.

Tense your hands—relax them.

Tense your throat—relax it.

Tense your face—relax it.

Always concentrate on how good it feels to be relaxed.

SELECTIVE RELAXATION

When you are in labor your uterus is going to contract and you must learn how to relax the rest of your body. You must learn to tense one part while relaxing the rest. The tensed part will play the role of the tense uterus.

1. Tense your right arm—relax left arm and both legs.
2. Tense your left arm—relax right arm and both legs.
3. Tense your right leg—relax both arms and left leg.
4. Tense your left leg—relax both arms and right leg.

Now imagine you are in the hospital in labor. You are in the labor bed and are beginning to experience your first contractions. Imagine a contraction starting. It is becoming stronger and stronger. Begin your slow deep breathing. Concentrate on keeping your body relaxed. Check your hands, arms, feet, legs, shoulders, throat and face. Imagine the contraction getting even stronger, and concentrate even harder on your relaxation and deep breathing exercises.

When your labor actually starts you will be able to remember your relaxation exercises and you will be able to control your body. Remind yourself that relaxation means a shorter labor, less pain and more oxygen to your baby.

BREATHING DURING LABOR

In addition to relaxation breathing, you will need to know some controlled breathing techniques. Breathing is the most natural thing you do during labor. Unfortunately, if you hold your breath or cry out, you will make your labor longer, become more exhausted and have more pain and discomfort—and you sure don't want that!

That wasn't too hard, was it? Now let's make it a little more difficult:

1. Tense right arm and leg—relax left arm and leg.
2. Tense left arm and leg—relax right arm and leg.
3. Tense both legs—relax both arms.
4. Tense both arms—relax both legs.

You are getting pretty good at relaxing your body while parts of it remain tense. Let's try one more exercise:

1. Tense right arm and left leg—relax left arm and right leg.
2. Tense left arm and right leg—relax right arm and left leg.

Controlled breathing, like relaxation, will help you to:

- Shorten your labor.
- Be more refreshed during your labor.
- Be more calm and in control during your labor.
- Have less pain and discomfort.

- Get more oxygen to your baby during labor.

Controlled breathing is easy to learn and most helpful during labor. You need only remember to:

- Concentrate on relaxation during your breathing.
- Match the breathing pattern to the intensity of your contractions.
- Always start each contraction with a deep relaxed breath and end each contraction with a deep relaxed breath.
- Be sure you breathe in a slow and relaxed pattern that is comfortable to you.

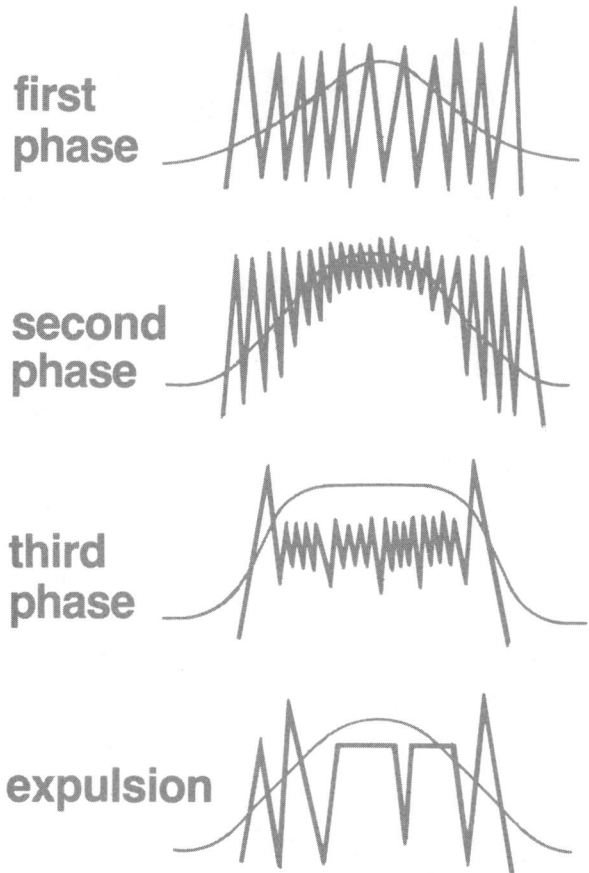

BEGINNING AND ENDING BREATH: You are going to begin and end each contraction with a deep breath (like a great deep sigh). Breathe in a deep breath through your nose (with your mouth closed). Now let out the breath with a great sigh.

SLOW BREATHING: While your contractions are just beginning you are going to need only a comfortable slow deep breathing pattern. Imagine you are having a contraction of sixty seconds. Begin the contraction with a deep breath. Now take in a deep slow easy breath through your nose while counting 1,2,3,4,5. Now let the air out through your lips counting 1,2,3,4,5. This one breath should take from about six to ten seconds (depending on how fast or slowly you breathe). So, if the contraction lasts about sixty seconds you will have five to eight of these breaths per contraction. At the end of the contraction take in a deep ending breath.

LIGHT BREATHING: As your contractions become stronger and longer, you may find that the deep slow breathing will no longer work for you. You will find your breathing naturally becomes faster as it matches the increasing intensity of the contractions.

TRANSITION BREATHING: Toward the end of your labor your contractions will become very strong, and you will have an overwhelming desire to push. You will find that the previous breathing patterns no longer work. Another type of breathing, blowing out air through your mouth in short puffs, will help you through the most difficult part of these contractions.

When you attend childbirth classes, breathing techniques will be taught in detail and you will have the opportunity to practice them before the birth.

THE COACH

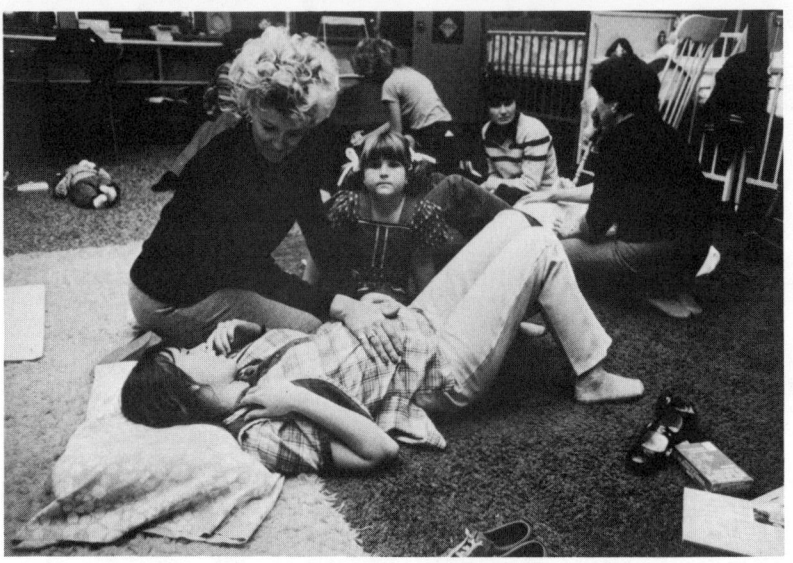

A coach is a person who helps a mother through her labor and delivery. The coach can be a husband, a friend, a mother or any supportive person. The coach will be able to give the mother great comfort and encouragement. As the labor goes along it is common for the woman to experience various discomforts as the baby moves down through her pelvis to the birth canal. Many of the techniques that the coach will learn will not only give the mother comfort during childbirth but can also give comfort to any person who is suffering from stress or pain.

PRESSURE:

Abdomen: Massage and stroking are the most comforting things a coach can do during labor. A light stroking on the mother's abdomen may give her great relief. Cup your hands and place only your fingertips on both sides of her pubic bone. Gently stroke up the sides of the uterus. Although this is usually great, if the mother has an irritable uterus, she may not like it.

Small of back: Place the heel of your hand on the small of the mother's back and apply steady pressure. She may like you to make circular movements.

Sacrum (lower back): You can also relieve back pressure by placing your fists on both sides of her sacrum (upper part of the tailbone). Apply steady, strong pressure in circular motions.

Coccyx (tailbone): As the baby's head descends, it may place tremendous pressure on the mother's coccyx or lower backbone. Deep back massage and pressure will give her great relief.

Shoulders and Neck: Massage her shoulders and neck and stroke down her spine to help her relax.

Buttocks and hip joints: Massage the buttocks and joints as if you were kneading bread.

POSITION:

Be sure the mom changes positions throughout her labor. Have her change from lying to sitting to lying on her side. She may even get relief from walking about. A warm shower may feel good (Go in with her; don't leave her alone.). If she is feeling a lot of back pressure, get her on her hands and knees to get the weight of the uterus off of her back.

COACH'S CHECKLIST:

To help the mother find the most effective breathing for her, use these key words:

- Even: Ask her if her breathing is even.

- Slow: Ask her if her breathing is comfortable. (If not, ask her to slow down and relax.)

- Rhythmic: Ask her if she has found a comfortable rhythm. (If not, count 1,2,3 with her.)

- Individualized: Ask her if she is dizzy or short of breath. (Help her slow her breathing down and count with her to make it even.)

- Comfortable: Ask her if her position is comfortable. (Help her to relax her throat and shoulders.)

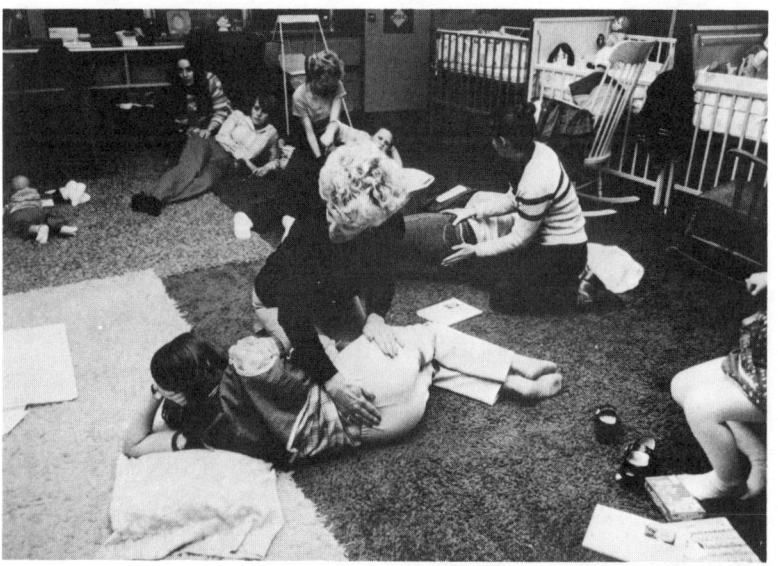

- Relaxed: Ask her if she feels relaxed. (Remind her to concentrate on breathing in warm, relaxing air and breathing out tension with each exhalation.)

TEMPERATURE:

Sometimes a hot washcloth, towel or heating pad gives the mom relief. If heat doesn't work, put ice chips in an icebag or a washcloth and apply it to the area that hurts.

Always remember to ask the mother what feels good and what works. Remember, what was effective one moment may not work the next, and what did not work the moment before may work the next.

Pure routine: things for the coach to remember

POSITION:

- Always ask the mother if she is comfortable.
- Help her avoid lying on her back, for this may impede blood and oxygen flow to the baby.
- Watch to see that her spine is straight and she is not cutting off blood to other parts of her body.
- Place pillows around her arms, legs, thighs, back, etc.
- Remind her to change her position every half hour.
- Be sure you yourself are in a comfortable position that is not fatiguing.

URINATION:

- Remind her to urinate every hour. The pressure on her bladder will desensitize her to the need to urinate.
- Remember to urinate yourself.

RELAXATION:

- Remind her to do conscious relaxations during each contraction.
- Remind her to relax between contractions.
- Use touch and verbal commands to help her relax.
- Remind her that tension will prolong her labor.

COMFORTING TOOLS TO TAKE TO THE HOSPITAL:

Heat: washcloth or hot water bottle for backaches

Cold: icebag, for cramps and aches

Cornstarch or cocoa butter for massage

Chapstick, mouth spray to refresh breath

Toothbrush, toothpaste to refresh mouth

Lollipops, sour candy, tea, sugar (or honey), popsicles to refresh and give liquid

Paper bag to breathe into in case of hyperventilation (and pack snack in for coach)

Warm socks in case feet get cold

Watch with second hand for timing contractions (if they are regular)

Books, cards, et cetera, in case you arrive at hospital in early labor

Paper and pencil to make notes and document contractions

Camera, film, flashes if you wish to take pictures

Snacks for coach: sandwiches, thermos of juice, coffee, et cetera

Coaching book

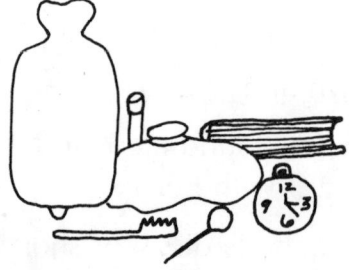

EXPULSION

Finally your baby is ready to make its journey down the birth canal. Your baby comes down through the cervix, into the vaginal canal, through the pelvic floor, and out the external opening.

POSITION:

Since the beginning of mankind, squatting has been the most used position for pushing out the baby. Although you probably don't want to squat in labor, you can learn a lot from the position and put it to use to make your delivery easier.

Get in a squatting position and feel the different parts of your body. Start with your head: Your chin is off your chest, your shoulders are rounded, your arms are bent out, your back is curved and your pelvis (bottom) is tilted. Whether you choose to deliver your baby *lying on your back,* in a *semi-sitting position,* or *on your side,* you can use these same techniques to have an easier, quicker delivery.

Semi-sitting: To assume a semi-sitting labor position, place pillows under your knees to give them a flex position, and enough pillows behind your head to lift you up. The small of your back should be pressing against the bed.

Side lying: Lying on your side during expulsion takes the weight of the uterus off your back. Prop your upper leg up with a pillow and extend your lower leg. This is the best position for delivery because your contractions are more efficient and you feel the least amount of pain.

WHAT CAN GO WRONG

PASSAGEWAY: Although usually your baby's head is made to fit perfectly through your pelvis, sometimes your baby's head may be larger than your pelvis. If this happens, a cesarean is the best thing for you and your baby.

PASSENGER: Sometimes your baby may decide to come out of your uterus in a position other than head first. If his feet, buttocks or shoulders come first, your doctor may have to use instruments such as forceps. Sometimes a cesarean is necessary.

POWERS: If your contractions are ineffective, weak, or infrequent, or if your uterus does not dilate or open sufficiently, you may require some kind of medication.

CESAREAN

"Cesarean section" means that the doctor makes an incision (or cut) about four inches long (usually right above your pubic bone). He then makes an incision into the uterus, puts in his hand and draws out the baby. The whole procedure takes just a few minutes and is a simple and fast way to have a birth.

After the doctor delivers the placenta, the incision is closed with special clips so you will hardly have a scar. You are taken to a recovery room right after the birth to be sure that you are doing well. Your baby is taken to the nursery to be sure that he or she is breathing well.

THE BIRTH OF MY BABY:

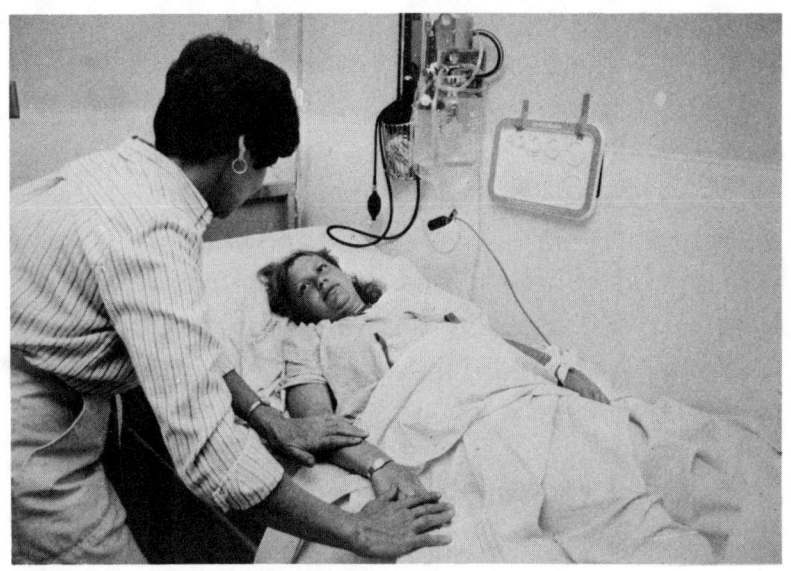

6:00 PM. *I had had contractions for about three hours. I timed them, but they were not regular. They were strong and then they let up. I ate a light dinner and took a walk. When I went to the bathroom I noticed that I had a lot of mucous mixed with blood.*

10:00 PM. *At about ten my contractions were getting more regular. They were about five minutes apart and they were getting stronger.*

12:00 A.M. *I called the hospital and told them that my contractions were three minutes apart and that they were very strong. They told me to come to the hospital. I called my coach and she came to pick me up. I was so scared but there was no turning back.*

1:00 AM. *When I got to the hospital they gave me an examination and found that I was completely effaced and that I was three centimeters dilated. They put me into a little gown that didn't do much for modesty. I was really getting excited about the birth.*

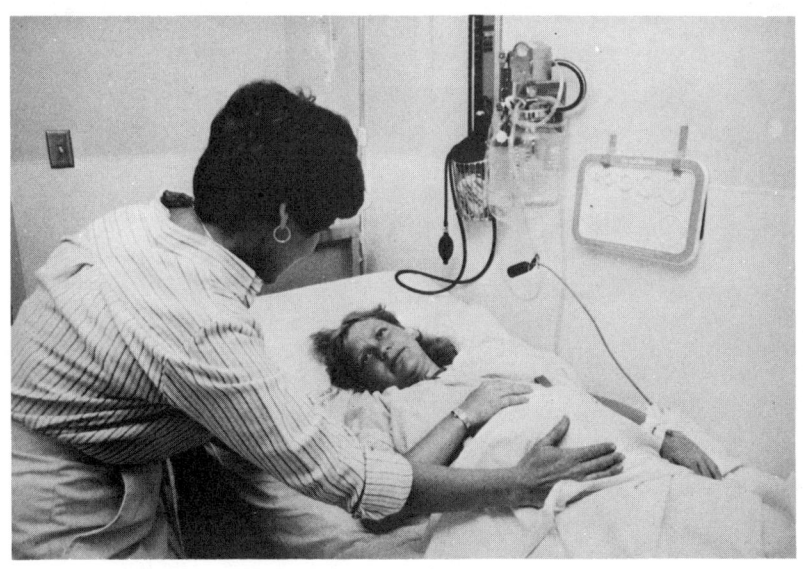

2:00 AM. *My coach and I started to do the deep, slow breathing and my coach did the massage that felt so good.*

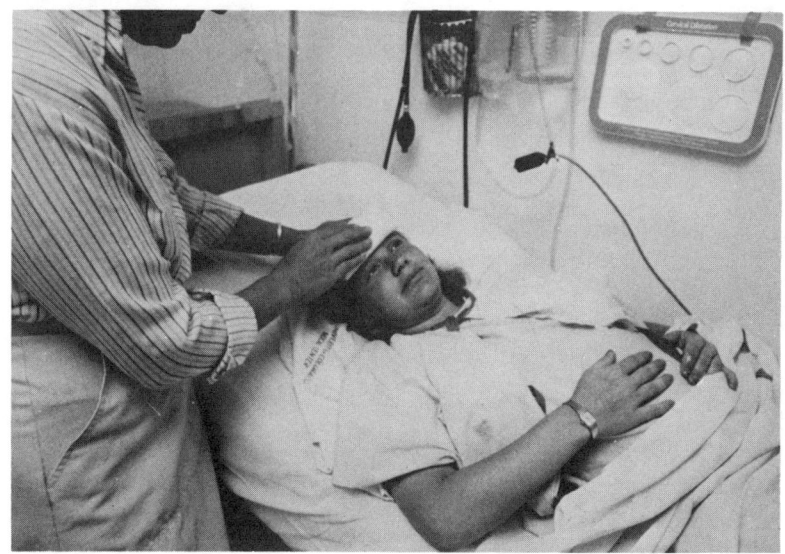

3:00 AM. *They checked me again and I was four centimeters dilated. My contractions were coming a lot stronger and longer. I wasn't so sure of myself now.*

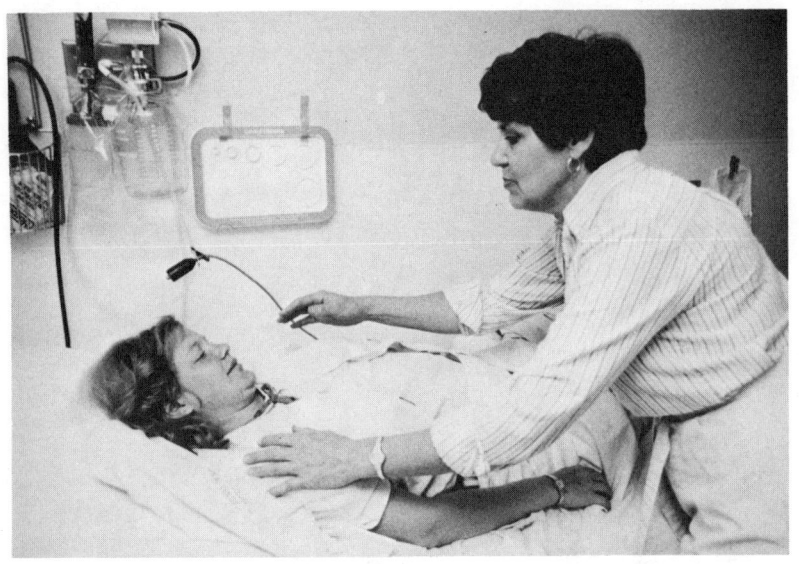 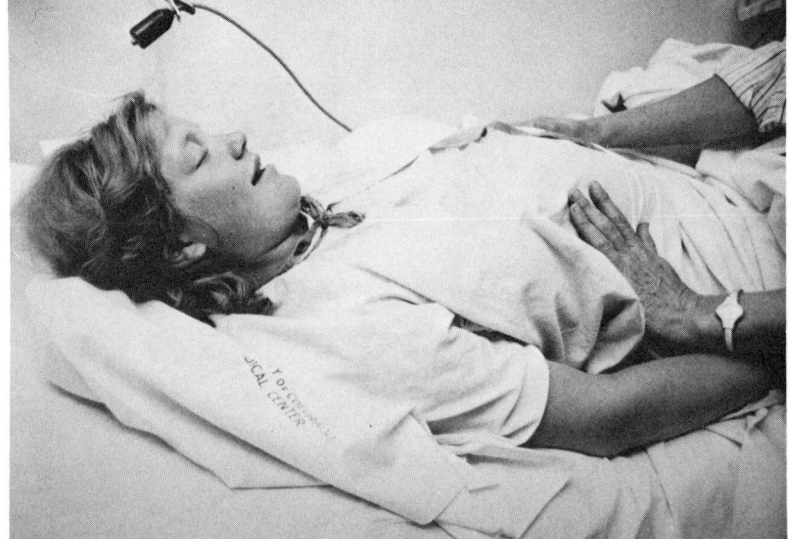

4:00 AM. *When they checked me again I was five centimeters. I never dreamed labor would be so hard. The contractions got harder and harder to work with. My coach helped me with my breathing and relaxation. I couldn't have done it without her.*

5:00 AM. *Some of the contractions came right on top of each other. It sure wasn't like the ones we learned in class. My coach kept reminding me that if I tensed up I would make my labor longer. That was the last thing I wanted.*

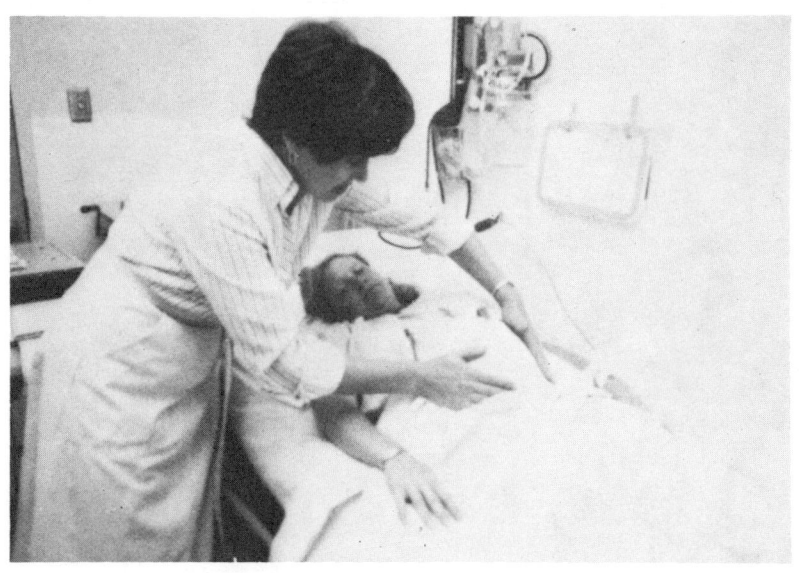

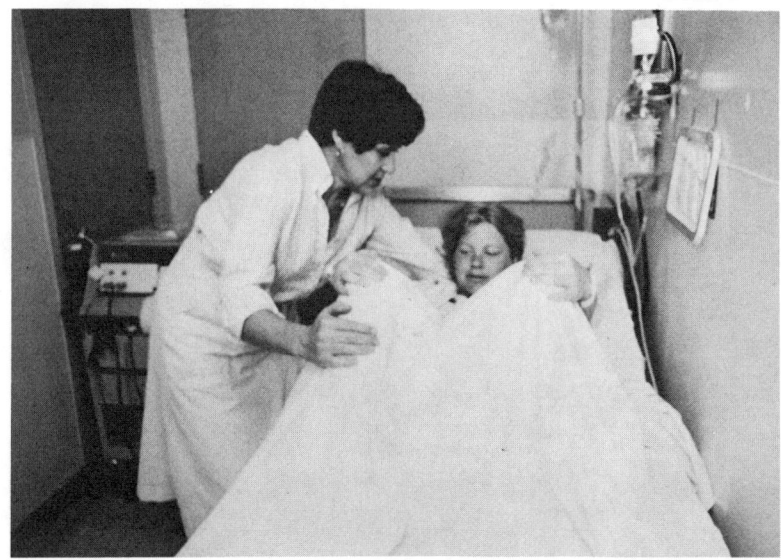

6:00 AM. *It was really funny—I suddenly got a strong urge to push with one of the contractions. My coach called the nurse and she said that I was in transition. The baby had moved down and it wouldn't be long before my baby would be born. She told me to pant so I wouldn't push quite yet. That was the longest period in my life.*

7:00 AM. *The nurse said I was completely dilated (my uterus was completely opened) and that I could begin to push. My coach helped me. I pushed for about an hour.*

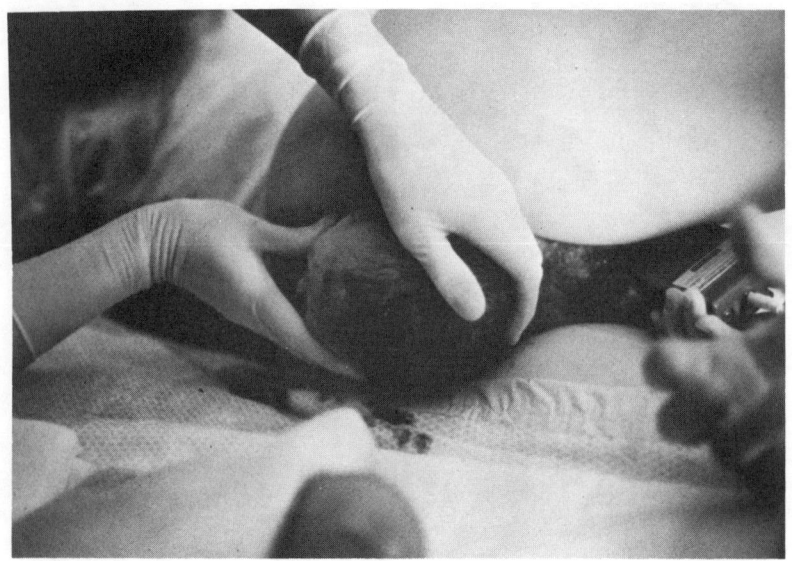

8:00 AM. *They took me into the delivery room, and I pushed some more. They told me to keep my eyes open. I could see a little of her head and then some more and some more. Finally, when the doctor told me to stop pushing as her whole head just popped out. He then told me to push just a little more and her whole body came out. She was born at 8:30 AM.*

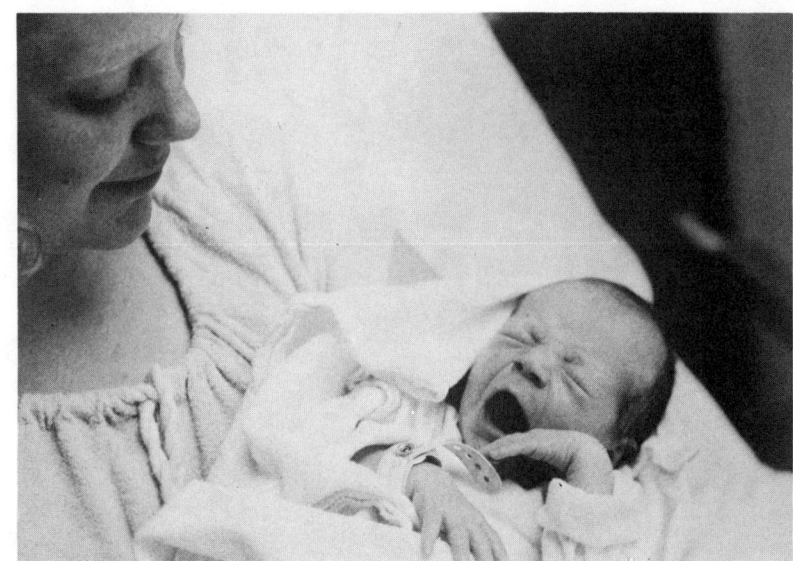

8:30 AM. *When they put her in my arms it was the most beautiful moment of my life.*

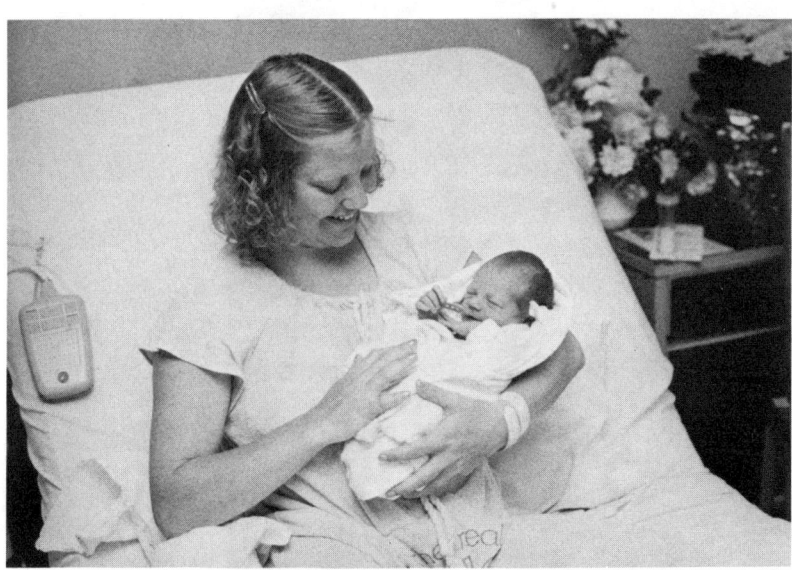

Who Is Going To Parent Your Baby?

CHALLENGE:

Once you find you are pregnant, your most important decision is: "Who is going to parent my child?"

CHOICE:

The choice you make—to marry the father, to be a single parent or to relinquish your baby to people who cannot have their own children—will affect you and your baby for the rest of your lives.

QUOTE:

"I'm scared that I might not be able to be mature enough to raise a baby. I'm worried about how I'll be able to support it and how my family is going to treat me and my boyfriend after it is born."

QUESTIONS:

What choices do I have?

How can I make a decision?

What are the pros and cons of getting married?

What are the pros and cons of single parenting?

What are the pros and cons of relinquishment?

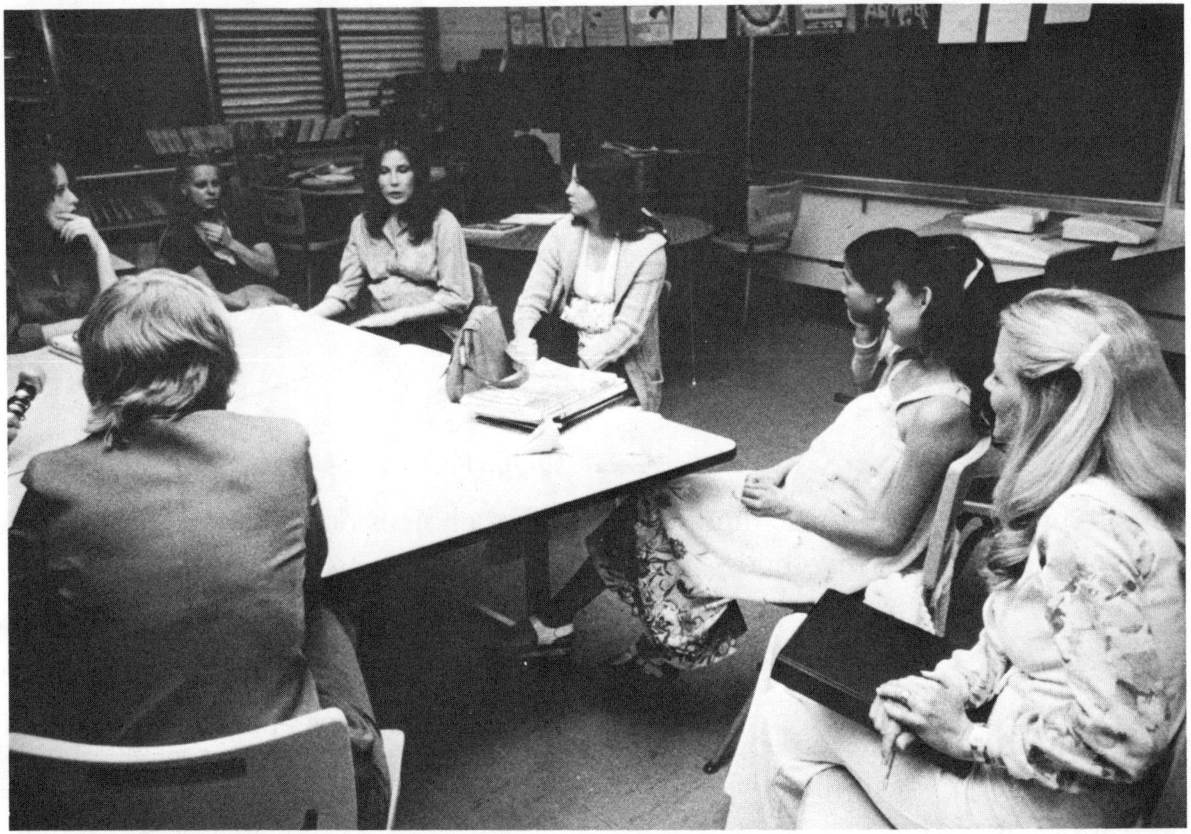

WHAT CHOICES DO I HAVE?

If you are not married, your choices are, of course, quite different than if you are married. You may choose to marry the father of the baby. You may choose not to marry and to single parent your baby. Or, you may choose to give your baby up for adoption. The father of your baby may have feelings of commitment and responsibility. Before you make such an important decision, it's important that you explore all the possibilities.

HOW CAN I MAKE A DECISION?

The decision you make will not be an easy one and it won't be a perfect one. But, it will be one that you and your baby will live with for the rest of your lives. We wish to share with you some of our experiences and our decisions and some of the questions we asked ourselves before we made the final choices.

PARENTING ALTERNATIVES

Out of 540,000 babies born to teenage mothers last year,

- four out of ten mothers were married.
- three out of ten married shortly after the birth of their babies.
- three out of ten chose not to marry.
- ninety-four percent of these mothers chose to keep their babies.
- eighty percent of all teen marriages ended in divorce.

Each of the alternatives—marriage, single parenting or relinquishment—is a form of parenting. Each carries with it advantages and disadvantages you should know.

what I did to mine. It would have been impossible, of course, me as a mother at 13, but I'm still sorry about it and I don't want to do it again.

Kimberly: *Mark and I have been going together since I was 14. When I got pregnant the first time, he said, "No way, no way you can have a baby at your age. You're too young and you will ruin your health. So, I got an abortion—but I still have some scars left. When I got pregnant this time, we got married because neither one of us wanted another abortion.*

ALTERNATIVE: ABORTION

It would be unrealistic of us not to include abortion as an alternative for some teens. Even though several of us had had previous abortions, all of us chose not to abort and were faced with other alternatives.

Angela: *I was going to have an abortion since I was only 15, but my family talked me out of it because of their religion. I love my baby now, but I'm only 16. I feel like I'm still only a child—and here I have a child. It's completely changed my life. I look at other 16-year-olds and know that I can never be like them again. I sometimes wonder if an abortion wouldn't have been better.*

Tammy: *I had an abortion when I was only 13 and it was a terrible experience. I look at other babies now and think*

ALTERNATIVE: MARRIED PARENTING

Pros:

Tina: *Marriage is good. I can depend on my husband financially, because he's the kind of man who will work. It's good because he gives me support and he gives the baby support. My husband takes care of the baby every night when I get home and have to fix dinner and do homework.*

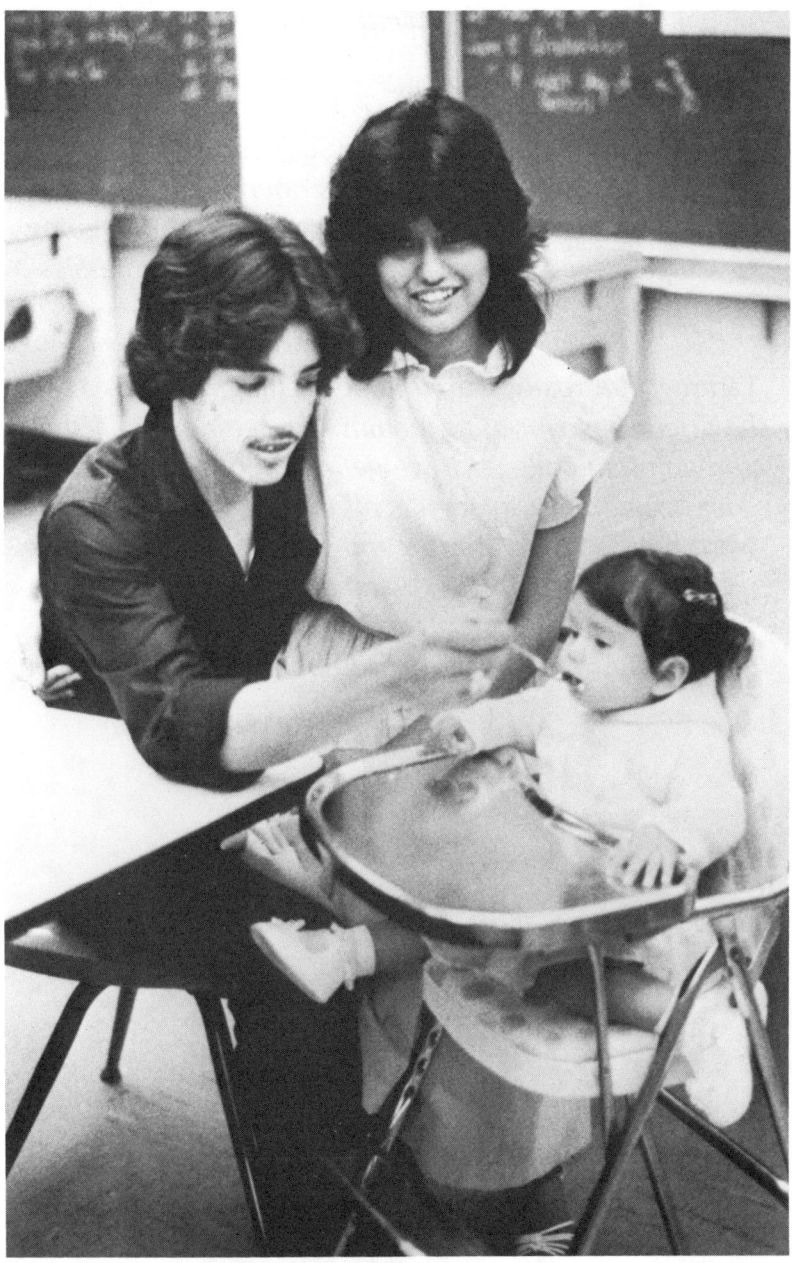

Molly: *The role of a father is really important. I feel for the people who don't have a guy around to help. When the baby is sick, my husband gets up with her; otherwise, I would never make it in the morning if he didn't help me half the time. And, when I am trying to cook dinner and she is cranky, he helps me. I think it's really important to have a father.*

Kimberly: *I think it's good for a child to have two parents. I think a little boy really needs a male role model. Having divorced parents is hard. I know from experience. I don't wish that on any little child.*

Cons:

Theresa: *Well, the biggest problem with marriage is the times you don't get along. There are a lot of things that you want to do and that he wants to do, and you just can't do them. A lot of guys are real possessive of their wives, and their babies, and that doesn't work out too hot.*

Kimberly: *I think one thing that I really hate is when we are fighting and the baby's there. That's not good for the baby at all.*

When the problems get really bad, you fight over who is going to have the baby. The baby is the one who gets torn apart. Just think about it: it's the baby who has to suffer for the parents' problems. Another thing I hate is when I come home at night, after school, and I'm exhausted. I'm tired, and I don't want to do anything. I have to think, "Oh, God, supper. Mark's going to be home and I've got to do the dishes and they've both got to be fed and then I have homework."

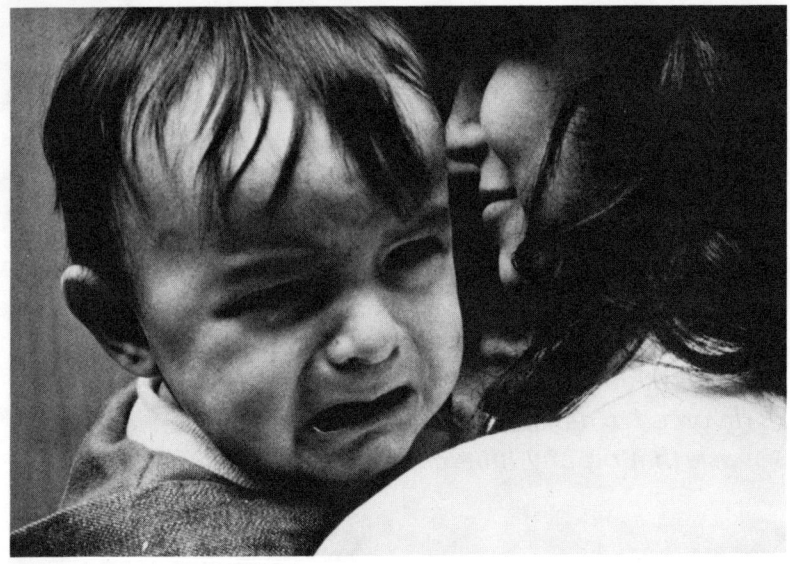

ALTERNATIVE: SINGLE PARENTING

Pros:

Nancy: *One big advantage to being single is your freedom. Husbands are really possessive. If you look at another guy, he's going to jump on you, "Don't do that! You're married to me."*

Holly: *I didn't want to have to hassle with the demands of a husband and a baby because the father is so demanding. He's almost like a child himself. So I didn't want to have to deal with both of them.*

Maria: *My boyfriend wanted to get married from the beginning. But I didn't know whether I wanted to or not. He is real sure of himself. But it's too scary for me. I know without my mom and dad I couldn't handle this. I'm not in a rush to get married and I'm not in a rush to get my boyfriend married.*

I'm glad I'm single because all I have to think about is feeding the baby, feeding myself, and doing homework, and that's it. There's nobody else to feed, nobody else to keep company. Your husband is going to want to have a conversation and tell about the hassles at work and you've got to listen.

Tammy: *I'm really scared about getting married. My boyfriend has a lot going for him, like getting scholarships and going to college. If we get married and something goes wrong, he can say it's all the baby's fault. I don't want him to feel closed in and feel like he had to give up everything he's always wanted. I know we both made a mistake but it's different for me. I didn't plan to go to college after I graduated. I wouldn't want for us to get*

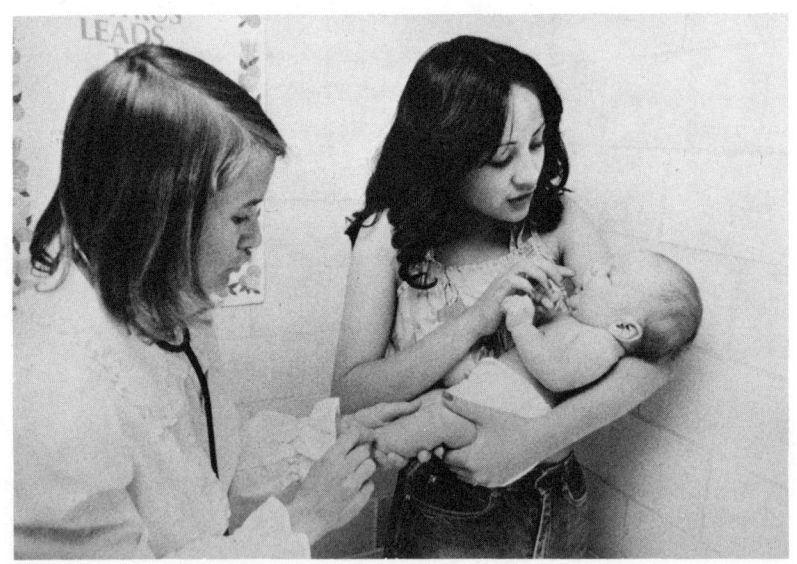

a divorce and hate each other. I would rather have us not married at all and both have the baby. I don't want to feel guilty and I don't want the baby feeling guilty.

Holly: *It will be a lot easier for me if I'm a single parent because the father is one pain in the rear end. I think the finances are okay because he's going to have to pay child support. It's going to be hard for me to be both a mother and a father. Later on he's going to wish he hadn't done all this. He's just as responsible for the child as I am.*

Cons:

Holly: *If you're married, you have someone to love and someone to take the baby. Being single, you don't have anyone to do things with or to love or to show that he loves you. You have to give all your love to the child, and you don't get any back right away.*

Maria: *I can't stay out as late as I'd like because I have to come home and take care of my child. How do you tell your dates, "I have a child already"? My child comes before them—how are they going to take that?*

Nancy: *When I'm by myself, it's really hard, because I have no time to think unless I call up some of the family members and say I'm going nuts. It's especially hard when the baby is sick because there is no pleasing her. You try everything twice. You are just about ready to pull out your hair sometimes. They are teeny and they don't know how to tell you.*

ALTERNATIVE: RELINQUISHING YOUR BABY

Pros:

Christina: *Relinquishing your baby is a form of parenting too. My parents let me decide if I wanted to keep the baby or not. I decided that I would not keep the baby because I'm not in any situation to take care of it financially and my parents aren't able to take care of another person. I couldn't take care of it without living on welfare and that doesn't sound like a good way to take care of a baby.*

Rebecca: *I did some thinking about the baby and the baby's future. I figured it would be better off with a couple*

that could keep it and take care of it. The adoption agency screens all the couples and I figured the kid would get a real good home.

Maria: *It gives people who care, a mother who can't have a child, an opportunity to have a little baby. And that's great. You know the baby's going to somebody who's trying so hard to get a little child. More than likely it's going to be loved and taken care of.*

Rebecca: *You can give the baby up and think, "My baby's happy and people really want it." You make so many people happy. If they love that child, they're going to give it love and a good life and money and all that stuff. And if they want it that badly, then it usually works out.*

Cons:

Holly: *I don't think I could live with giving up my child. The rest of my life I would wonder what it looks like, and how it is doing.*

Kimberly: *I think as the kids got older it might be harder on them because they would think, "Well, why didn't my mom want me? Was it because she just didn't want me, or because she couldn't support me, or..." There's going to be that time of depression.*

Maria: *I think making the decision that your child is not going to be happy with you and giving it to someone else is the hardest thing you can ever go through. You have to believe that she'll be better someplace else. I think it takes a lot of courage to do that.*

SOME QUESTIONS TO ASK YOURSELF BEFORE YOU MAKE A DECISION

It may help you to ask yourself these questions before you make a final decision. The answers won't be easy but they may help guide you in what's best for you and what is best for your baby.

MARIAGE:

- Do I love the father and want to spend the rest of my life with him?
- Will he make a good father?
- Is he mature enough to make a go of marriage?
- Am I mature enough to make a go of marriage?
- Will marriage make schooling more difficult?
- Do we have enough money to live on?
- Do we fight a lot? Would he ever hit me or the baby?

SINGLE PARENTING:

- Would it be easier to parent the child by myself?
- Will my parents help me?
- Do I have enough money for food, clothing and rent?
- Where can I stay with the baby?
- Who will take care of the baby when I am at school or at a job?

RELINQUISHMENT:

(Questions you need to ask yourself if you're considering keeping your baby).

Your Baby's Needs:

Do I have the physical strength to take care of a new baby twenty-four hours a day (that means 12 p.m., 2 a.m., 4 a.m., 6 a.m.)?

Do I have the patience and skills for a crying baby?

Do I want to stay home and babysit or would I rather go out?

Do I know what to do when my baby gets sick?

Do I want the responsibilities of cooking, shopping, cleaning and washing clothes and diapers (every day)?

Your Own Needs:

Am I ready to give up my independence for a twenty-four-hour-a-day job for the next eighteen years of my life?

Will I be able to finish school?

Will I be able to get some vocational skills for a career?

Do I want to give up the social life and friends I had before my pregnancy?

How will the baby fit into my social life?

(Questions to ask yourself if you're considering relinquishing your baby.)

Am I mature enough to give my baby to other parents?

Would I be able to pick up my life where I left off?

What if my parents do not want me to give the baby up?

What if the baby's father does not want to relinquish the baby?

What will my friends think if I relinquish my baby?

How can I find an agency that I trust to find the best family for my baby?

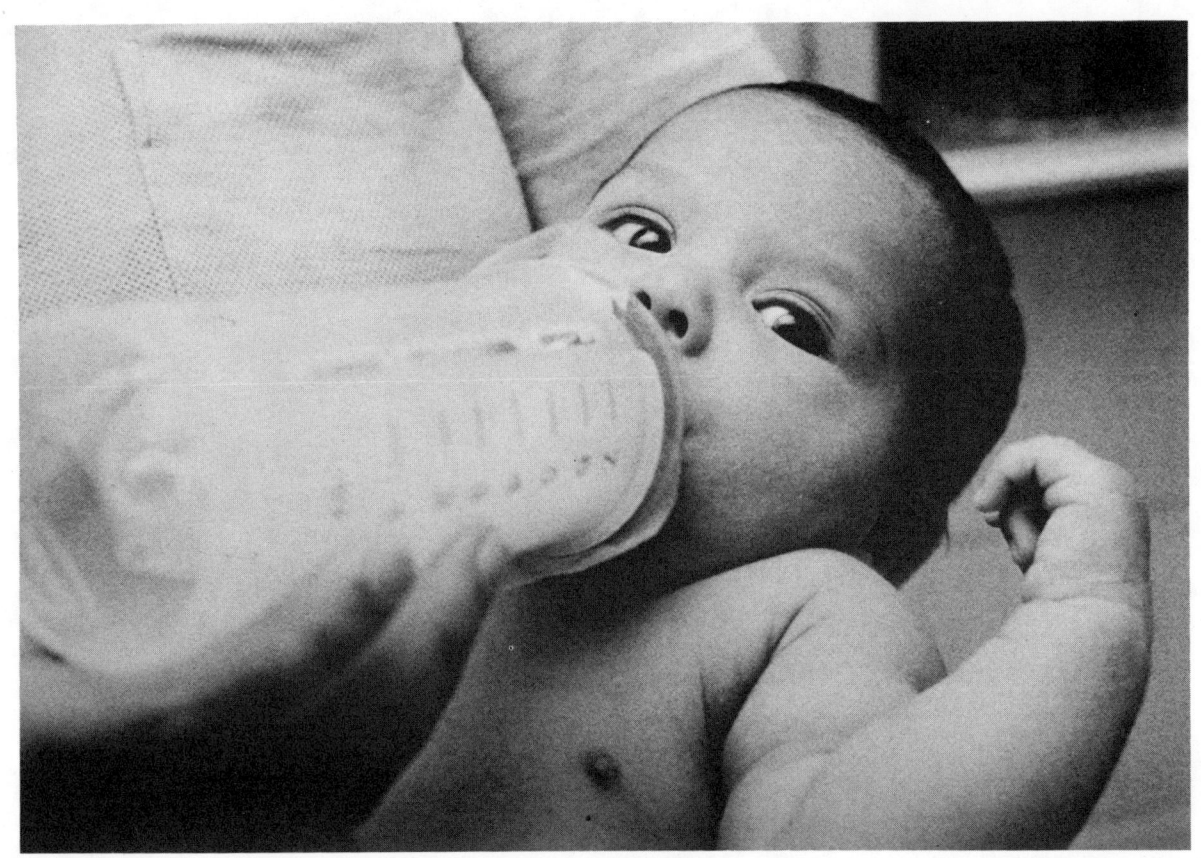

Parenting: What Do You Do With A Newborn?

CHALLENGE:

Those of us who kept our babies were unprepared for a baby's twenty-four-hour-a-day needs. Common problems that all new parents have were twice as bad for us.

CHOICE:

We who chose to keep our babies all wanted to be good mothers. What we needed most of all was information on how to take care of a baby, how to feed and comfort our babies.

QUOTE:

"Parenthood is for eighteen years of your life. When the babies are little, it's little problems, like getting up at night when they are sick. It is twenty-four-hours-a-day. When they get sick, you have to be there. You can't ignore their problems. And then, as they get older, it's bigger stuff. It's not just when they are little that it's hard—it's until forever."

QUESTIONS:

What kind of a parent am I going to be?
How do I show my baby I love him?
How do I soothe my baby when he is crying?
Can you spoil a baby?
How do you play with a new baby?
How do you feed a baby?
Why should I breastfeed?
How do you burp a baby?
When should I call the doctor if my baby is sick?

HOW OUR BABIES CHANGED OUR LIVES

Nobody could have ever told us how new babies would change our lives. Not one of us was prepared for it.

Kimberly: *Before the birth, I could give my husband attention all the time. It was a new adjustment with the baby there, crying and needing to have its needs met. Financially, the baby was one more big expense.*

Nancy: *My baby was colicky so she kept me up every night. I wasn't prepared for that. I just said "Oh, my poor baby, she must have a terrible stomach ache," and I'd just sit there. I'd have to be up with her every half hour.*

Tina: *My biggest concern is to make sure I do everything right. I want to do something when I'm supposed to be doing it and not do something else that is wrong. I don't have the information I think I'm going to need for a new baby. When I ask my mom about things, she says, "Oh, I don't remember." She says she can't remember back 18 years ago.*

Angela: *It's not all fun and games being a parent. It's important to consider that you may not only ruin your life but you are also responsible for ruining a little tiny person's life. If you can't get your act together for yourself, do it for that little baby.*

Rachel: *I thought having a baby wouldn't be very hard. But getting up at night and taking care of him while he's sick and having to give up a lot is the reality of it. I didn't think it would be as hard as it is.*

Nancy: *It's hard leaving them with babysitters when you want to go out. I used to feel guilty about leaving her. Changing diapers all the time gets old. I thought it would be different. I thought it would be like playing dolls—but it's not. It's work. It's 99 percent WORK.*

Angela: *The baby cries and cries and cries. And you can't comfort it. And you get so that you lose all of your maturity, you lose all of your patience. You cry, you're angry.*

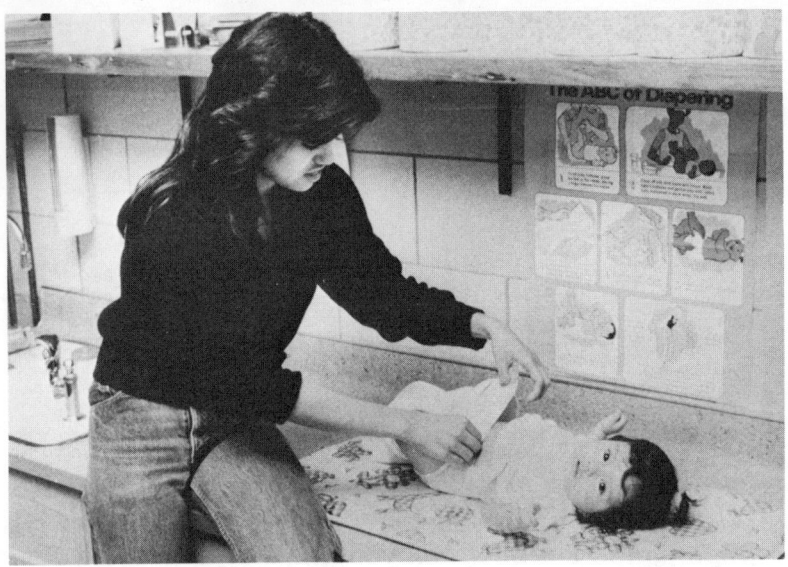

Nancy: *If you are alone and don't have parents and grandparents to help you, it's a terrible stress to have a baby twenty-four-hours-a-day. You won't know it until you do it.*

Robyn: *Stephanie has colic all the time and she's going to have it until she's three months old. I felt like I was a bad mother because she had it. I'd pick her up and I'd just want to say, "Would you shut up?" There's nothing you can do.*

WHAT KIND OF A PARENT AM I GOING TO BE?

Everyone wants to be a good parent. But wanting is not enough. You might think that parenting is an instinctual thing and that you automatically will know how to parent. Nothing is further from the truth. Parenting is really a learned skill, and if you choose to keep your child you will need lots of information, skills and support to be able to be the good parent you want to be. Your first lesson in what kind of parent you are going to be is how your own parents raised you. You can choose to do those things you like in how they parented you, and you can also choose to avoid those things you did not like in the way they parented you.

Love Your Baby

The most powerful lesson you can give your baby is to love him. Kiss him, talk to him, sing to him, touch him, soothe him, tell him you love him again and again. You are teaching him that you love him and you are teaching him how to love others. You are the

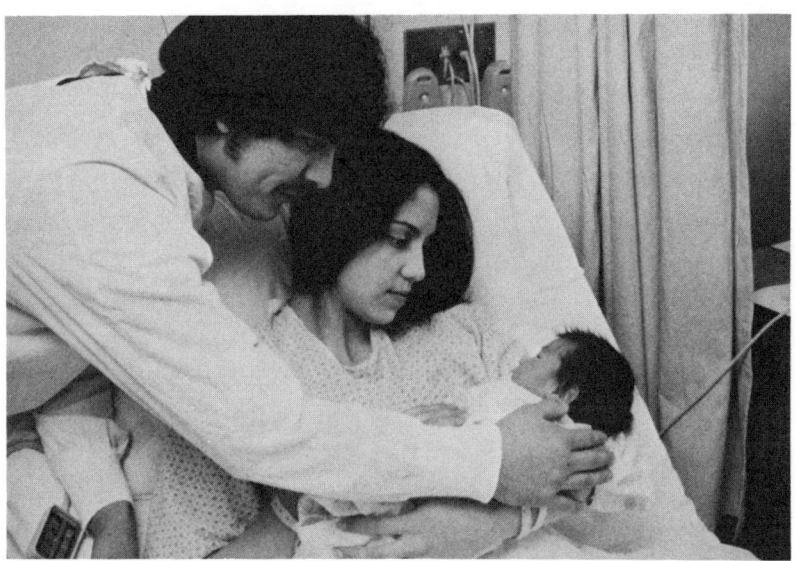
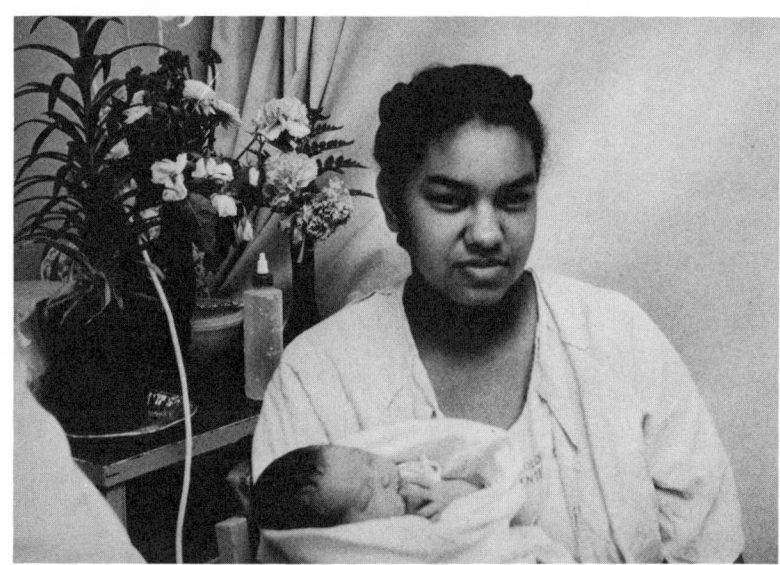

only person who can teach him this most important first lesson in life.

Soothe Your Baby

Your baby is a tiny human being who has one means of getting your attention: crying. He is not a tyrant trying to ruin your life. He is just trying to tell you of his needs. The most important thing you can do is respond to your baby's cry. In fact, the more quickly you respond to his cry, the less he will cry. The less you respond, the more he cries. You cannot spoil a new baby.

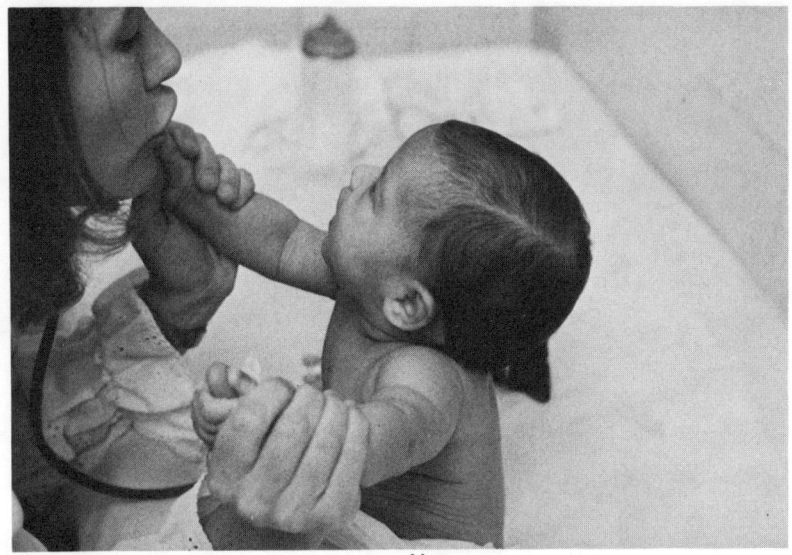

Play With Your Baby

Hold your baby, cuddle him, croon to him and talk to him. Your baby prefers your face above all others. There is nothing that pleases him so much as when you play with him. Hold, cuddle, sing, and talk to him. It doesn't make any difference what you say. In fact, research shows that the more you talk to your baby when he is young, the better he will be in reading, writing and arithmetic in his later school years. Your baby loves brightly colored objects and loves to have you point things out to him. He loves mobiles and moving things.

Feeding Your Baby

Next to loving your baby, the most important thing you have to do is feed your baby. Whether you choose to breastfeed or to bottlefeed, you will need information, skills and support. The important thing about feeding your baby is HOW you feed him. Each feeding time is a lesson of love and you should plan to give him all the cuddling, holding, and skin-to-skin contact you can.

BREASTFEEDING: If you choose to breastfeed your baby, there are several things you can do to have a successful time. First, you should prepare your breasts during pregnancy so that when your baby begins to feed, your breasts will be accustomed to handling. Second, you should plan to breastfeed your baby on demand. That means that nature has designed you and your child to fit each other's needs perfectly. When your baby signals that he is hungry, feed him. The more your baby sucks, the more milk your breasts provide. If you feed him frequently and let him nurse a long time, you have a much better chance at having a good milk supply for your baby.

ADVANTAGES TO BREASTFEEDING:

1. Human breast milk is the perfect food for human babies.
2. Breast milk gives your baby more resistance to infections, colds, flus and diarrhea.
3. Breastfed babies always get touching, fondling, cuddling and skin-to-skin contact.
4. The new mother returns to normal more quickly.
5. It is pleasurable for the mother.
6. Night feedings are much easier.
7. It is less effort.
8. Breastmilk is more economical.
9. The baby's stools are not smelly and odorous: they are light-colored and pleasant smelling.

BREASTFEEDING INFORMATION AND HINTS:

- Most babies need help in learning how to start breastfeeding.
- Always begin each breastfeeding session with the breast last used.
- Use both breasts at each feeding.
- It is common for a newborn to go to sleep during feeding. Wake her up.
- You may experience uterine cramping during breastfeeding.
- It takes time for both mother and baby to establish a successful routine.
- Breast milk looks thin, bluish, and watery because it does not have a lot of fat in it.

Burping

To help your baby get rid of any excess air in her system, burp or bubble her after each feeding. The traditional way is to hold her up with her tummy near your shoulder and gently pat her back. You can also burp or bubble your baby in a sitting position, with one hand firmly on her stomach and the other patting her back. A little spitting up is perfectly normal. It usually occurs after a feeding and is caused by an air bubble. If your baby spits up a great deal, she may be overeating. Sometimes it helps if you burp her before the feeding, during the feeding, and after the feeding as well.

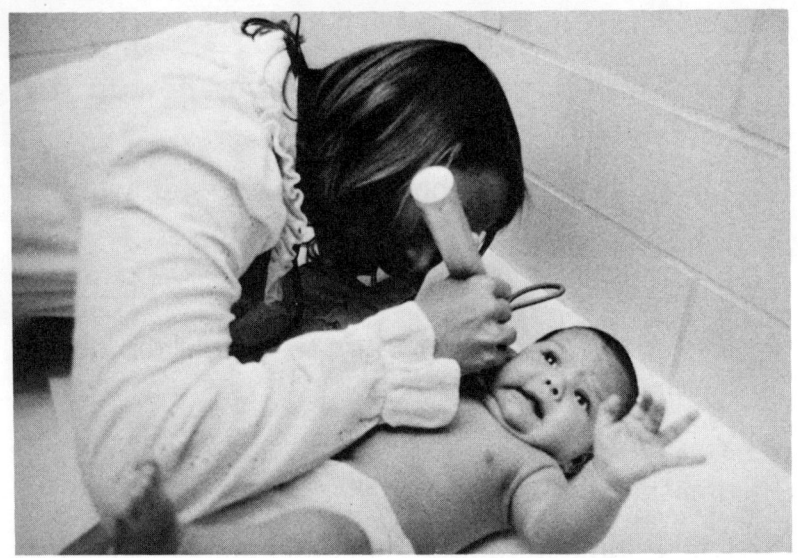

WHEN TO CALL YOUR DOCTOR

Every mother experiences moments when her baby is not feeling well. You know your baby better than anyone, and when she is not herself, you know it right away. Sometimes it is difficult, however, to decide when your baby's symptoms are severe enough to call your doctor. Below are some guidelines to follow, but whenever you become worried, it's best to call your doctor right away, simply to relieve your mind.

If you see the following behavioral or physical changes in your baby, let your doctor or clinic help guide you for your baby's safety. When you call, be sure to tell them what you have done in the way of food, medication or other treatment and how your baby responded.

Behavior Changes:

- Excessive crying: crying much more than usual with a change in color and appearance.

- Unusual irritability: crying, combined with an unusually high degree of irritability.

- Changed sleeping patterns: excessive drowsiness or unusually poor sleep patterns with waking and crying periods.

- Appetite: loss of appetite and continuous refusal to take food.

- Movement: listlessness, restlessness, and thrashing about.

Physical Changes:

- Elevated temperature: When your baby has a temperature of 101°F or more (98.6°F is considered normal), she may have a fever (although babies often run a high temperature simply as a result of lots of activity).

- Skin changes: When your baby has a flushed face, has hot or dry skin, is perspiring, or if she is pale and listless, she may be sick even though her temperature is normal.

- Repeated vomiting: Your baby throws up most of her feedings.

- Diarrhea: Your baby has stools that are watery or contain pus or blood, with loose, frequent bowel movements.

- Inflammation or discharge from the eyes: Although some babies develop a mild inflammation of the eye because of a blocked tear duct, redness or pus can be a sign of a problem.
- Congestion: Coughing, severe hoarseness, or a stuffy nose that causes difficulty in breathing can be an important sign.
- Convulsions: If your baby has a relatively high fever, she may experience convulsions. Although frightening, they are seldom dangerous and are usually over in a few minutes. Call your doctor immediately.
- Pain: When your baby cries in a high-pitched tone and is inconsolable, call your doctor.

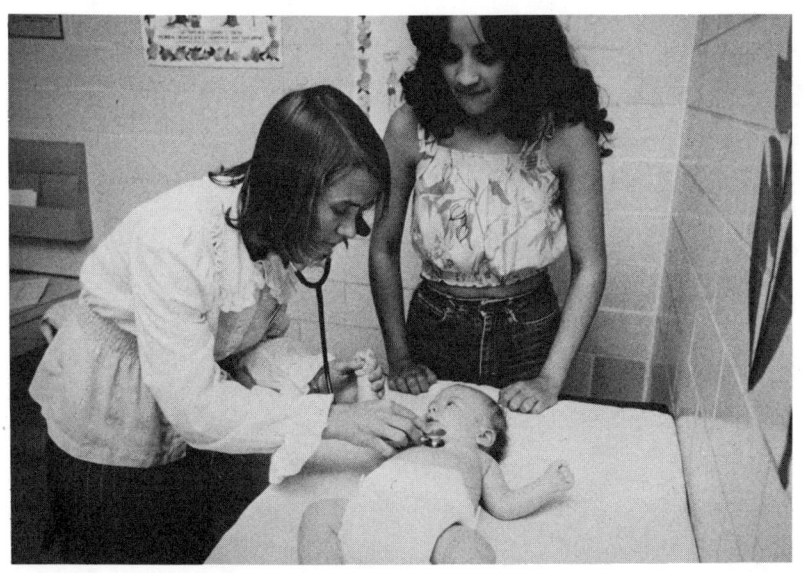

WHAT TO TELL YOUR DOCTOR

PHYSICAL CHANGES (How your baby looks)	**BEHAVIOR CHANGES** (How your baby acts)
My baby's temperature is _____.	My baby's crying is (excessive, high-pitched)
My baby's skin is (flushed, hot, dry, pale)	
My baby has vomited (between feeding, with unusual force)	My baby's behavior is (irritable, restless, miserable)
My baby's bowel movements are (color, consistency, odor and frequency)	My baby's sleeping is (prolonged, intermittent)
My baby is (coughing, sneezing, hoarse)	My baby's appetite is (poor, nonexistent)
My baby's eyes are (irritated, inflamed, discharging)	
My baby's movements are (abnormal, twitching, stiff, convulsed)	My baby's movement is (listless, restless, thrashing)

WHEN YOUR BABY IS SICK

Sleep and rest are important when your baby is ill. Keep the room quiet and dark and keep her away from people. Forget feeding and sleeping schedules and let her rest as much as possible. If your baby has a cough or stuffy nose, keep the room humid and warm, but not overheated.

If your baby has a fever, don't urge her to eat. When she is awake, offer her liquids or milk every half hour. If your baby vomits, let her stomach rest. Don't try to feed her, but give her some sterile water. If the water stays down and she wants more, give her a little at a time.

Use medication only when and in the amount your doctor prescribes. Give an enema only when it is prescribed. Do not use left-over prescriptions; throw them safely away.

If your baby has a fever, a wet rub or sponging may help to lower the baby's temperature. With a cool, wet sponge, rub each of your baby's arms, then each leg and finally her back. Take a few minutes to stroke each part.

Remember that when your baby is sick, she needs not only your physical help, but your sympathy, tenderness, and love.

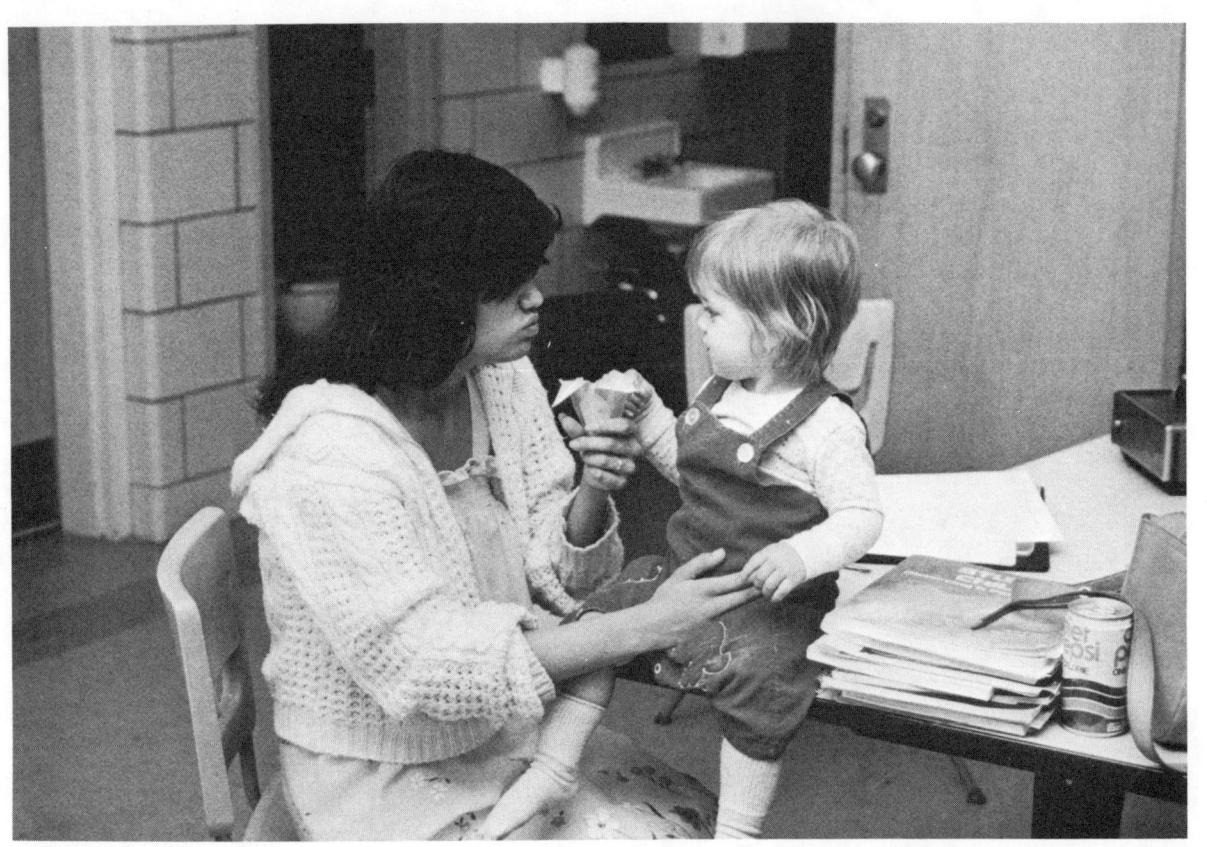

Pregnancy: You Do Have A Choice

CHALLENGE:

Eighty out of one hundred teen mothers who do not use any kind of contraceptives will be pregnant again within the next eighteen months.

CHOICE:

You have a choice in how many children you will have and how close together they will be born. This choice will affect your whole future: your marriage, your education, and your own children's future. You have a right to demand from your partner commitment, love, loyalty, support and a guarantee not to be abandoned with an unwanted child. You have the right to know about and use contraception.

QUOTE:

"Know what you want before you have sex. Give yourself a chance to plan things instead of letting them all happen at once. I didn't plan for any of this. It just happened and I'm sure that if I planned for it, it would have been a lot easier. And never think, 'Oh, it's not going to happen to me, so I don't need to worry.' You will be just like me. It's not hard to get pregnant."

QUESTIONS:

When should you have sex?

What are the most important things in a relationship?

How can I say "No" and still keep my boyfriend?

How can I say "No" and still get someone to like me?

How do I know when it's the right guy?

How can you tell if a guy is handing you a line?

How can you say "No" to a line?

What kind of contraception will work for me?

What is the easiest contraception?

What is the most effective contraception?

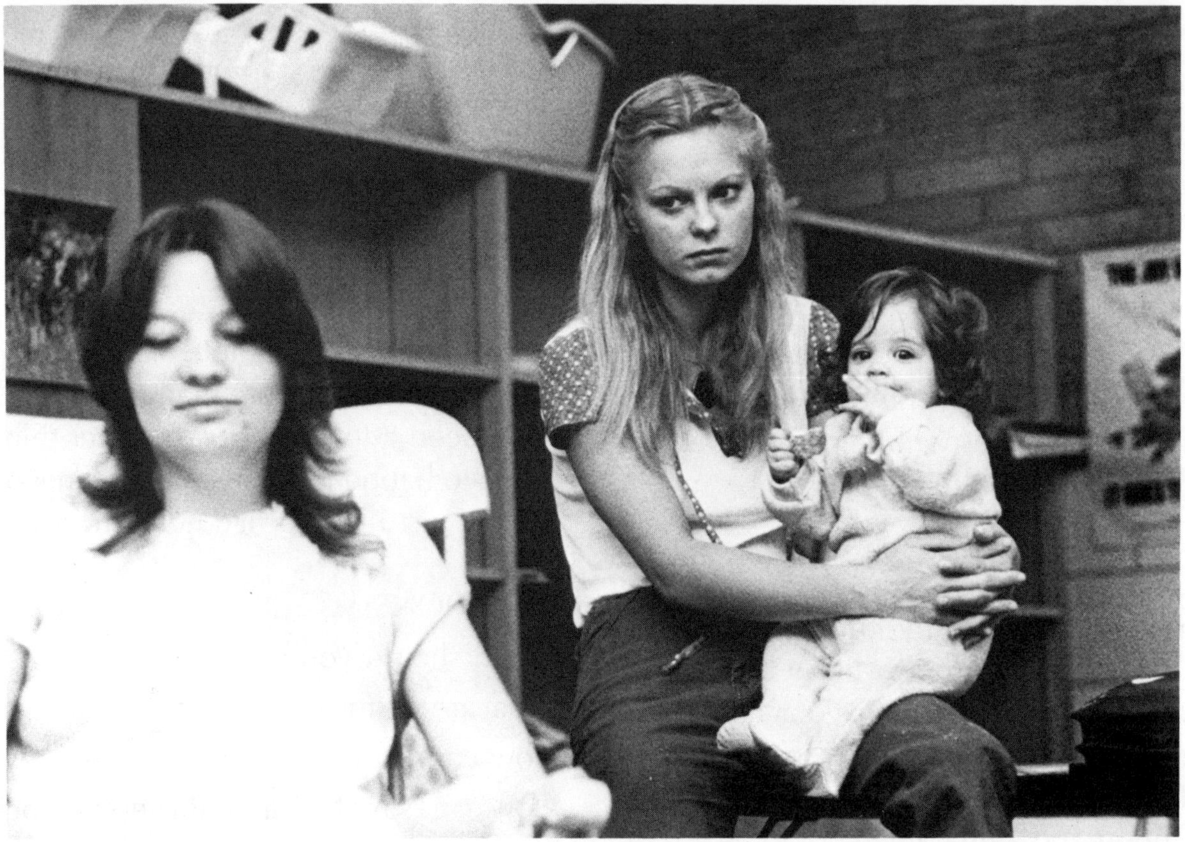

WHY WE HAD SEX

We think it is important to understand the reasons that a person might decide to become sexually active. Although several of us were married, we had all had sex before marriage. Each of us had her own story and her own reasons for beginning sex.

A lot of us found that we had become sexually active for a lot of reasons that had nothing to do with love or sex. Some of these reasons were:

CURIOSITY: "All of my friends were having sex and I was curious to see what it was all about. I didn't even know the guy very well and I don't even want to know him now. It wasn't like it is shown on TV or in the movies. I didn't even enjoy it."

PEER APPROVAL: "All my friends were doing it and they dared me. After all, I was seventeen and had never had sex. I thought maybe I really was missing something. (I wasn't.)

TO ESCAPE FROM HOME: "All we ever did was fight, fight, fight. I was sick of school and when I got pregnant I got out of the house and out of school. I'm married, have a baby and am much happier now than I have been before in my life."

TO COMBAT DEPRESSION: "My life really doesn't have much hope. I don't do very well in school; my parents are divorced. I really don't have much to look forward to. Maybe this baby will bring me some happiness."

REBELLION AGAINST PARENTS: "I was tired of being treated like a baby by my parents. 'Do this and do that. Be home by eleven o'clock.' I used sex to prove to my parents and to myself that I really am an individual. But now I'm more dependent on them than ever. I want to move away and take my baby but I don't have any money. My dad told me that if I move out, I have to leave my baby."

THE ONE-LINERS THAT GOT US PREGNANT

Many of us didn't want to have intercourse and we certainly didn't want to get pregnant. We found that we fell for a lot of different lines. Some were convincing, some were funny, and some were stupid but they all got us pregnant.

Most of us were so trusting that we believed the guys when they said they loved us and "if we really loved them we would…." We found out later that they only told us that to get us to have sex with them.

We'd like to share with you some of the lines that got us pregnant so that other girls might not be as innocent (and dumb) as we were.

My boyfriend told me that if God gave us the desires they must be good and I believed him. Now I see him in church and he won't even talk to me.

Ricky promised me I wouldn't get pregnant because during sex he would take it out before the sperm came. I tapped him on the shoulder and said, "Ricky, did you forget something?" Because he got so excited he forgot and here I am.

I didn't use anything because my boyfriend told me that he had had and operation and that there was only a 50 percent chance he could father a baby. We only had intercourse once—and you're looking at the 50 percent.

My boyfriend told me that he was too young to have a baby and I believed him. Can you believe that?

My boyfriend told me that it was selfish of me to hold myself back when I could give him so much pleasure. I believed him. Now I have a baby and he has another girlfriend.

HOW CAN YOU TELL IT'S A LINE?

If your boyfriend tells you that it's the only way you can prove your love—it's a line.

If your boyfriend threatens to break up or leave you if you don't have sex with him—it's a line.

If your boyfriend tells you that sex won't end in pregnancy—it's a line.

If your boyfriend can't talk to you about contraception ("It's not romantic")—it's a line.

If you don't know your partner well enough to ask him if he's had any contact with venereal disease, you're probably falling for a line (and may very well end up with VD).

Remember, the only contraceptive that really works 100% is saying "No." If you can't (or don't want to say "No") the next best contraceptive is saying "Yes" (each and every time) to some kind of birth control device. Believe us—sexual intercourse ends in pregnancy. We know it because we've got the babies.

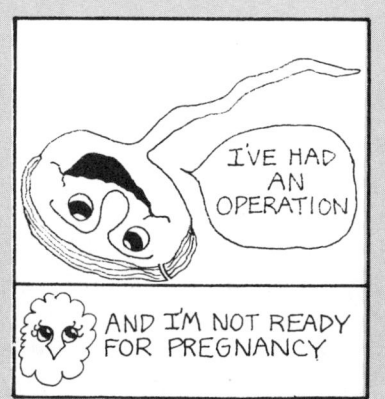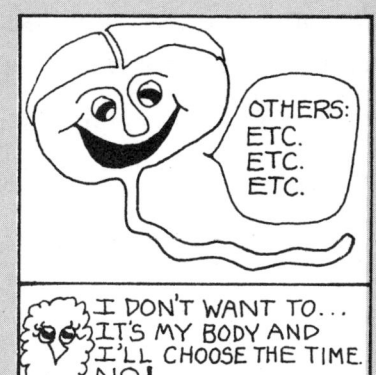

LINES TO SAY NO:

If you're old enough to have sex, you're old enough to be a father.

God not only gave us the desire to have sex but the ability to be mothers and fathers.

There is a million to one chance that I will get pregnant each and every time we have sex.

Pulling out in time is one of the best ways to get pregnant.

There is no 'safe' time.

If you loved me, you wouldn't pressure me into having sex when I'm not ready for it.

If you would leave me if we don't have sex, I guess you would leave me if I got pregnant.

It's against my religion.

I really don't feel like it.

If our relationship is dependent on sex I guess we don't have much going for us anyway.

I'm not ready for pregnancy.

I don't want to.

It's my body and I'll choose the time.

No!

Since the beginning of mankind, guys have been working on gals to go to bed with them. Our point is: it's girls, not boys, who get pregnant and end up with the babies.

It's we who suffer the most. And, although some of us were married and some of the fathers did marry us, most of us were abandoned by our boyfriends. They said things like, "I'm not the father." Lines like, "How do I know it was me?" or "Somebody else must be the father—who have you been sleeping with?" really hurt.

MESSAGE TO OUR TEEN SISTERS

Nancy: *Be picky about the men you date and the man you choose. If you get pregnant and you're dating a guy who's not going to stick around, it's a mess.*

Theresa: *That goes the same for boys, they should be more selective about the girls they go out with because what if a girl is just trying to trap you? I'm sure there's girls like that. And they should watch out for them. If she's a real runaround, you don't even know if the kid is yours. And she just wants to marry you. She'll just say "Oh it's yours," and half the time she doesn't know either.*

Kimberly: *If you're fooling around with a guy who doesn't care about you, stop. It's one thing if your boyfriend cares about you and you get pregnant. If he's just fooling around and doesn't care about you, forget it.*

Robyn: *Some girls will have sex to get guys to like them. Some girls do it thinking, "Well, I'm going to keep this boyfriend." If I could, I would tell them, "Don't, until you feel they respect and love you." You're too good to be chasing and trying to make someone stay with you.*

Rebecca: *Make sure the guy is not immature. If he is, he's not going to be able to take on the responsibility of a baby and he's not going to want to have that baby around. You also have to make sure that you know him real well.*

THE MOST IMPORTANT THINGS WE WANT OUT OF A RELATIONSHIP

LOVE: Caring for one another

COMMUNICATION: Being able to communicate with each other

FUN: Having fun and being able to laugh together

CARING: Genuinely caring about each other

FRIENDSHIP: Having a close and caring friend

EMPATHY: Having a person who understands you

TRUST: Having someone you can trust

FREEDOM: Giving each other room

ROMANCE: Having someone you can have fun and romance with

Angela: *I want someone I can love and who loves me in return. I want to care for him and I want him to care for me.*

Maria: *I want to be able to communicate with my boyfriend. I want to tell him how I am feeling and I want him to tell me his feelings too. When we have problems*

I want to work them out instead of getting mad at each other or not talking to one another for a week.

Rachel: *I want a man who will understand me and won't laugh at my thoughts. I want him to know when I am sad or disappointed and I want him to care about how I feel. I want him to accept me the way I am.*

Susie: *I want a guy who will support me. When I told the father of my baby that I was pregnant, he told me the kid wasn't his. Now, I've got a baby and I've got a $6000 hospital bill to pay back to my parents and he's taken off with someone else. The next guy I'm going to look for is going to have the maturity to accept his responsibilities.*

Tammy: *I want a guy who trusts me and isn't jealous of every move I make. My boyfriend has no reason to be jealous of me. (In fact, he's the one who has had the affairs!) But, he still acts as if I am trying to make out with every guy. I ask him, 'Hey, Ricky, who wants me now—with a baby?'*

Theresa: *The thing I miss and need most is freedom. When your husband is jealous, you feel like you are in jail. You have so much responsibility that it presses down on you. I want the freedom of trusting my husband and his trusting me.*

Robyn: *Sex and romance are fun. I don't mean always going to bed, but the fun of going places together—holding hands, kissing, learning to know each other better. Those are all important to me.*

SUMMARY: We all decided that we are all pretty nice people. We care and are loving toward people. We are nice to be around and have a lot to bring to a relationship. We decided that we are all pretty special and we deserve pretty special guys. We decided that we were going to have to like and respect ourselves before we could ask guys to respect us.

We decided that when a guy can't give you love, can't care about you and won't support you, you shouldn't be having sex with him. Nobody knows better than we do—you can (and we did) end up pregnant.

HOW DOES BEING SEXUALLY ACTIVE AFFECT YOUR LIFE?

For those of us who are married, sexual intercourse is a romantic and meaningful part of our marriage. For those of us who were not married (and for some of us who *were*), intercourse ended in unwanted pregnancies. When you are sexually active, you have to worry about contracting diseases like syphilis, gonorrhea and herpes. You have to think about difficult issues like abortion. If you are sexually active (married or not), you have to worry about effective contraception. (And although all of us thought we were using some kind of contraception you can still get pregnant if you don't know how to use it right.)

IF YOU DO CHOOSE TO BE SEXUALLY ACTIVE AND YOU DO NOT WANT TO GET PREGNANT, YOU MUST:

1. Admit you are having sex.
2. Admit you will continue to have it.
3. Admit you don't want to get pregnant.
4. Get help from a person or place knowledgeable about contraceptives.
5. Understand that using contraceptives without knowledge and information can end in pregnancy.
6. Learn how to use contraceptives properly.
7. Use contraceptives EACH AND EVERY TIME you have sex.
8. Understand that having a baby is a 24-hour-a-day job, seven days a week, 52 weeks a year, for the next 18 years of your life.

WHAT KIND OF CONTRACEPTION WILL WORK FOR YOU?

No contraception except saying "No" is 100% effective and simple to use. You can increase the effectiveness of contraceptives, however, by understanding how, when and why they work.

To understand contraception you must understand conception. That's really quite simple. It only takes one sperm meeting one egg. Making love, sexual intercourse or having sex is the way that the sperm gets to the egg.

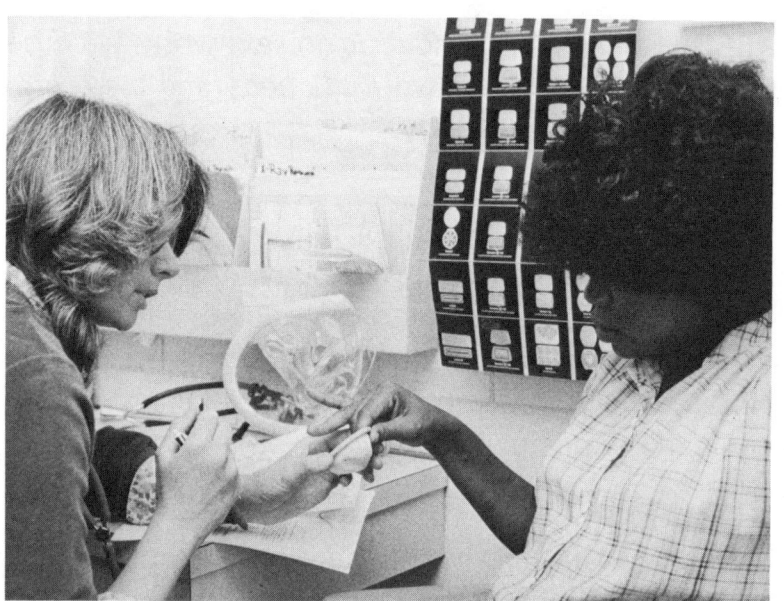

There are three ways that conception cannot take place:

1. If the sperm and egg remain apart by not having sex

    or

2. If some kind of barrier keeps the sperm and egg apart during intercourse

    or

3. If something prevents the fertilized egg from developing.

Unfortunately, Mother Nature does everything possible to get the sperm to the egg. Each and every time you have intercourse you could possibly conceive a child. You may hope and you may pray but unless you use some kind of contraception, you can't fool Mother Nature.

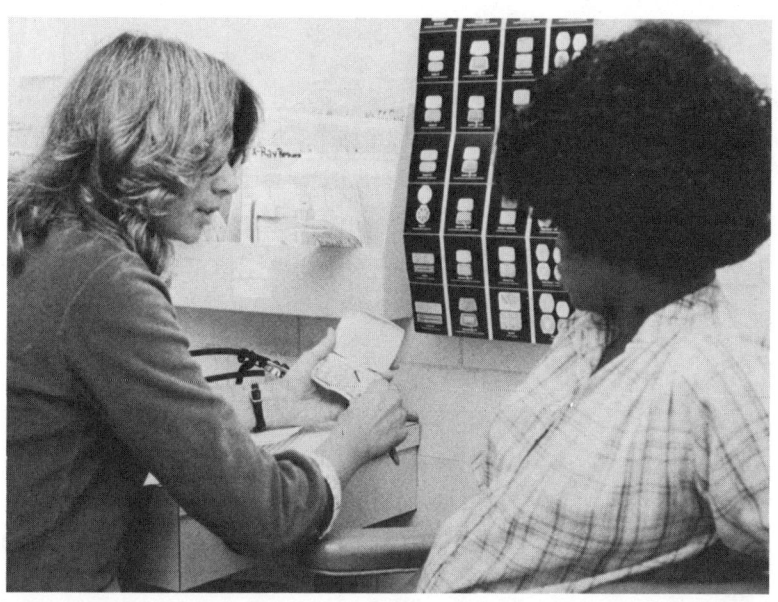

ABSTINENCE: Abstinence, or no sex, works because the egg remains in the woman's body and the sperm remain in the man's body.

THE PILL: The birth control pill works because the hormones in the pill fool your body into thinking that you are pregnant and your ovaries do not release eggs. When there is no egg, there can be no pregnancy. However, if you miss even one day of taking the pill, you can get pregnant.

THE IUD: The IUD works because it stops the egg from implanting into the uterus. If the egg passes out of your body, you cannot get pregnant. However, if the IUD comes out (and you don't know about it), you can get pregnant.

THE DIAPHRAGM: The diaphragm is put into the vagina against the cervix and acts as a barrier against the sperm. A jelly that kills the sperm is an added protection. However, if the diaphragm does not fit well, or if you remove it too early, you can get pregnant.

THE CONDOM: The condom, or rubber, covers the penis and catches the sperm, keeping them away from the egg. However, the condom doesn't work if it's used twice, if it's old and breaks during intercourse, or if sperm leaks out as the penis is removed from the vagina.

FOAM: Foams, jellies and creams are put into the woman's vagina. They make a barrier to block the sperm from entering the uterus and getting to the egg. They also kill the sperm. A new application must be used each and every time you have sex. Foam only lasts about an hour and if you have sex after an hour and do not use more foam, you can get pregnant.

RHYTHM BIRTH CONTROL: A woman for whom natural family planning works must be extremely tuned into her body. There is *NO* safe period unless a woman makes detailed charts of her periods and her temperature to determine when the egg is released during her menstrual cycle. She must have a partner who is willing to work with her to abstain from sex when she releases the egg. Rhythm does not work when a woman's periods are irregular or when a woman is not absolutely sure of the time when she ovulates.

METHODS THAT DO NOT WORK:

1. Douching with anything
2. Sitting or standing during sex
3. Breastfeeding
4. Withdrawal
5. Having sex during your period

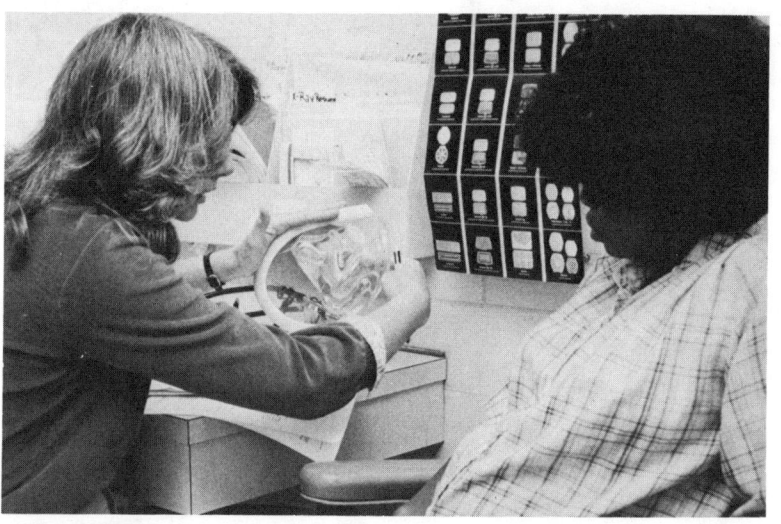

information

BIRTH CONTROL METHODS THAT REQUIRE A VISIT TO THE DOCTOR OR CLINIC:
- The pill
- The IUD
- The diaphragm

BIRTH CONTROL METHODS THAT DON'T REQUIRE A VISIT TO THE DOCTOR OR CLINIC:
- Foam
- Vaginal inserts
- The condom

THE BEST CONTRACEPTIVE FOR YOU IS:
- Reliable
- Prompt
- Confidential
- Free or low cost
- Easy to reach

CHOICES YOU NOW HAVE:
- Delay sexual activity
- Use a contraceptive device

RISKS:

No medical problems
- Abstinence
- Natural methods

Possible minor problems
- Vaginal inserts
- Diaphragms
- Condoms

Possible serious problems
- IUD's
- Pills

METHODS THAT DON'T WORK:
- Withdrawal
- Different positions
- Breastfeeding
- Menstruation
- Douching

BIRTH CONTROL METHOD EFFECTIVENESS

Method	Effectiveness
Pills	99.7 percent
IUD	97-99 percent
Condom	90 percent
Foam, cream and jelly	80-90 percent
Diaphragm	97 percent

FACT:
- You can get pregnant if you have sex standing up
- If you take birth control pills only when you have sex, you can get pregnant
- You can get pregnant while menstruating
- Douching after sex will not prevent pregnancy
- If you are breastfeeding you can get pregnant
- You can get pregnant if you have sex during your "safe period"

REASONS WE DIDN'T USE CONTRACEPTIVES (AND GOT PREGNANT BECAUSE OF IT):
- "I didn't expect to have intercourse and got caught without anything."
- "I didn't think I would get pregnant."
- "Contraceptives were not available to me."
- "I thought it was wrong to use contraceptives."
- "My boyfriend didn't want me to use anything."
- "I thought it would spoil the romantic mood."
- "I thought my boyfriend would think that I had planned to have sexual relations with him."
- "It was my first time and I didn't think I would get pregnant."

BEST PROTECTIONS AGAINST VENEREAL DISEASES
- Abstinence
- Condoms

(Pills & IUD's offer no protection)

VENEREAL DISEASE

Things to know:

One can be infected with VD without having any symptoms.

Most forms of VD can be cured if treated early enough.

The treatment of VD is by prescription drugs only.

There is no self treatment or cure sold over the counter.

VD can be acquired over and over again.

Birth control pills do not prevent or treat VD.

VD endangers not only the infected person but all people with whom the person has intimate contact.

A pregnant woman with untreated VD may pass it on to her fetus, with devastating consequences.

VD is not a disease of filth or dirt but of sexual activity.

The diagnosis and treatment of VD is confidential information.

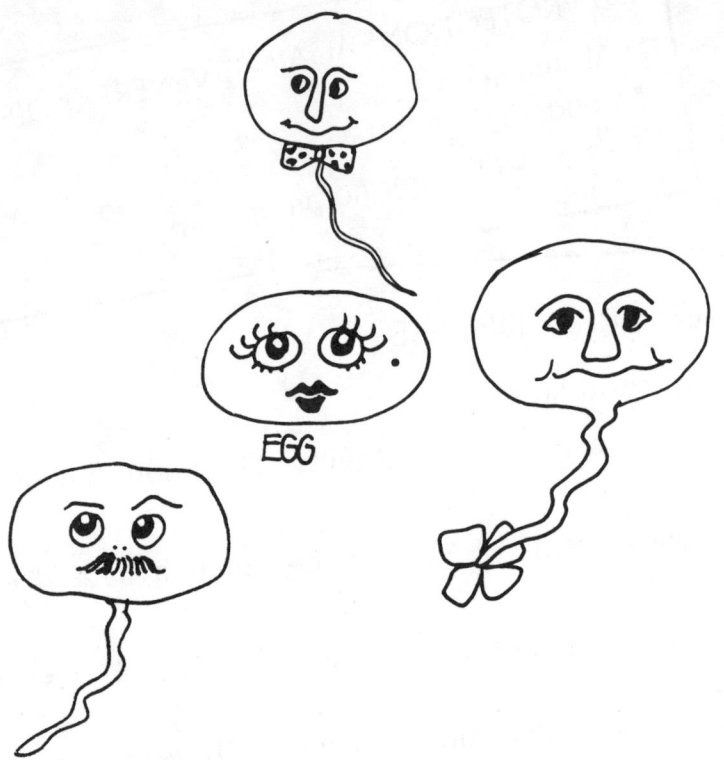

OUR ADVICE ON CONTRACEPTIVES:

Theresa: *I'd say even if you're married, don't get pregnant until you're older. It's a lot of responsibility. I was only sixteen and I had my whole life ahead of me. Now I have a baby and a husband, and there's a lot of things that I can't do.*

Nancy: *I'd say don't have sex until you're ready. And if you're going to do it, have some contraceptive device handy. If you are going to do something, do it with responsibility. Pregnancy is going to happen to you. Don't think, "It's never, ever going to happen to me," because it will.*

Maria: *Think about what you're doing before you do it. If you feel like you might have sex, make sure you have some kind of protection. Otherwise, it will lead to being pregnant. I did it only once, and I got pregnant. Everybody laughs because they think it's funny, but it's true.*

The Pill:

Kimberly: *I wish I had taken the pill. I waited too long. I just kept telling myself, "Well, I can wait a little bit longer." And then I found out it was too late. I wasn't afraid to take it—I just kept putting it off, and putting it off, and I put it off too long.*

Nancy: *I wouldn't have remembered to take a pill every day. I'm not even sure I could use the pill because my mother has high blood pressure and she can't use the pill. There are other forms of contraception like the IUD and*

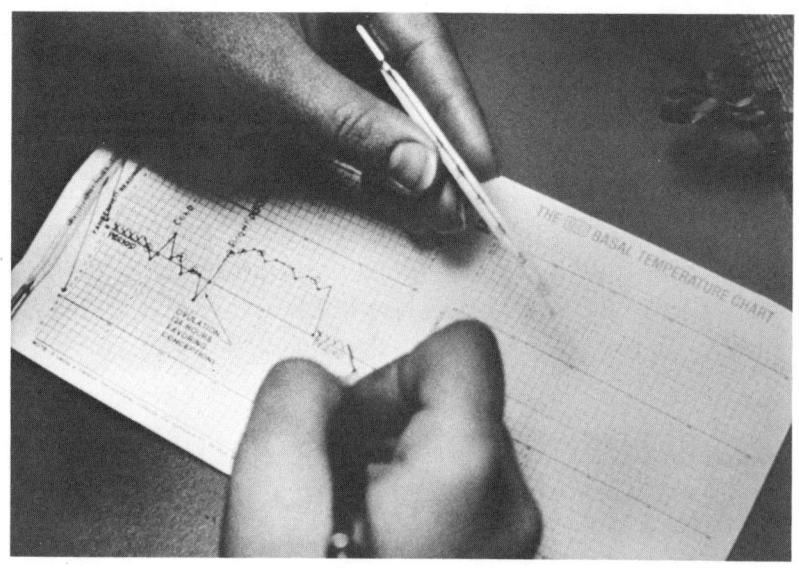
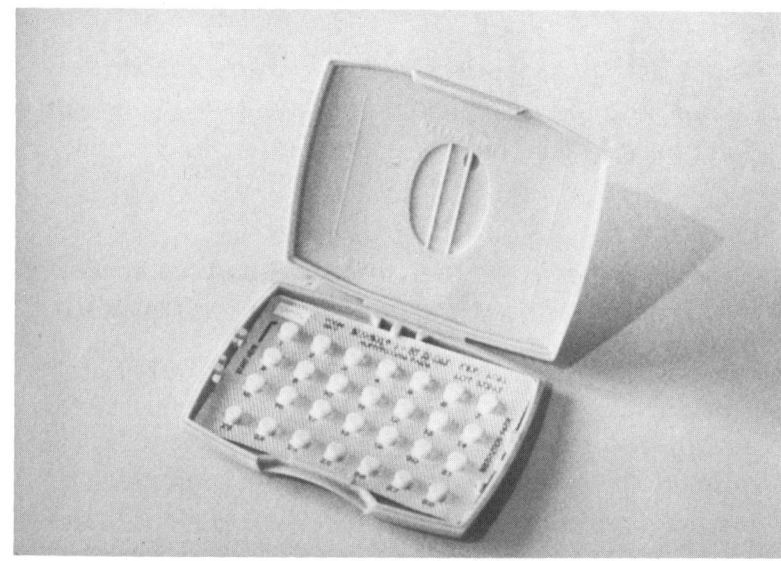

diaphragm. It depends on what you can or can't use and what you'll take the responsibility to use.

Tina: *Although the pill probably isn't the best thing for you as you get older, I think that while you're young, the pill would be good.*

Nancy: *I really think it depends on how often you have relations. If you are having relations regularly I think that the pill is the safest.*

Christina: *I was taking the pill and I had a stroke. My doctor found out I should never have been on the pill because my mom and her mom both have high blood pressure. I was on the pill eight months and the whole time it was affecting me negatively. You have to go to someone who really knows your past history.*

Tina: *If you take a pill, nobody is going to know or see it. I always keep it in my bathroom at home. I like the pill because when you are in the mood, you are in the mood. You don't have to stop because you have already taken the pill ahead of time.*

Angela: *You can't take the pill if you're breastfeeding.*

The Diaphragm:

Christina: *I think the diaphragm is best because you don't have to leave anything in your body. It's better than the pill because there are no chemicals left inside you.*

Holly: *I was using a diaphragm at the time I got pregnant. I must have done something wrong. I must not have put enough jelly or maybe I didn't put it in exactly in the right position.*

The IUD:

Nancy: *If I had a serious relationship with someone now, I would use the IUD. You don't have to stop and you don't have to take the pill every day.*

Condoms:

Nancy: *My boyfriend used condoms and we never got pregnant for two years. But one time the condom broke. It must have been an old one.*

Condom and foam:

Kimberly: *I make my husband use a condom and foam. We use them both together. I don't want to get pregnant again. Besides, it can be romantic if you do it right.*

Suppositories:

Holly: *I thought from the advertisements that those things would work. But something didn't work.*

Rhythm:

Robyn: *My boyfriend told me that if we had sex during my "safe period" I wouldn't get pregnant. But my periods were never exactly regular and I always figured halfway between periods. I've since found out that your fertile period is fourteen days <u>before</u> your next period. Now how am I ever going to figure out fourteen days before my period when I don't even know when my period is going to be?*

Abstinence:

Maria: *I'm using the contraceptive that works best for me: I'm not having any sex.*

Rebecca: *If I had thought about it twice, I wouldn't have done it in the first place. So now, when I'm going to do something, I'm going to think about it more than just once. I'm just not going to do it—it's not worth it!*

THE PILL

What it is
"THE PILL"
Pills with two hormones, an estrogen and progestin, similar to the hormones a woman makes in her own ovaries.

How it works
- Prevents egg's release from ovaries
- Makes cervical mucus thicker and changes lining of the uterus.

How to use it
Different types:
1. Take a pill a day for 3 weeks, stop for one week, then start a new pack.
2. Take a pill every single day with no stopping between packs.

You will get pregnant if you:
- Miss a day
- Take someone else's pills
- Don't use some other form of contraception for the first month
- Have severe vomiting or diarrhea

Advantages
- Convenient
- Extremely effective
- Does not interfere with sex
- May diminish menstrual cramps.

Disadvantages
Must be prescribed by a doctor. All women should have a medical exam before taking the Pill, and some women should not take it.
- Nausea
- Weight gain
- Headaches
- Missed periods
- Darkened skin on the face
- Depression may occur.
- Blood clots
- Strokes

Effectiveness rate:
Proper use:
99.7% if used consistently, but much less effective if used carelessly.

Poor use:
60%

DIAPHRAGM

What it is
DIAPHRAGM WITH SPERMICIDAL JELLY OR CREAM
A shallow rubber cup used with a sperm-killing jelly or cream.

How it works
The diaphragm fits inside the vagina. The rubber cup forms a barrier between the uterus and the sperm. The jelly or cream kills the sperm.

How to use it
You insert the diaphragm and jelly (or cream) each time before intercourse. It can be inserted up to 6 hours before intercourse and must stay in at least 6 hours after intercourse.

You will get pregnant if you:
- Leave the diaphragm in the drawer or anywhere other than your vagina.
- Don't insert diaphragm properly.
- Do not use spermicidal jelly each time.
- Use someone else's diaphragm.
- Are not refitted after the birth of a baby.

Advantages
- Effective and safe.

Disadvantages
Must be fitted by a doctor after a pelvic exam. Some women find it difficult to insert, inconvenient, or messy.
- Some women find that the jelly or cream irritates the vagina. Try changing brands if this happens.

Effectiveness rate:
Proper use:
About 97% effective if used correctly, and consistently, but much less effective if used carelessly.

Poor use:
80%

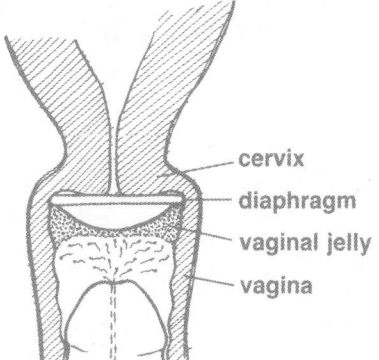

CONDOM (RUBBER)

What it is
CONDOM ("RUBBER")
A sheath of rubber shaped to fit snugly over the erect penis.

How it works
The condom prevents sperm from getting inside a woman's vagina during intercourse.

How to use it
The condom should be placed on the erect penis before the penis ever comes into contact with the vagina. After ejaculation, the penis should be removed from the vagina immediately before removing condom.

You will get pregnant if the man:
1. Does not put the condom on properly.
2. Uses an old condom.
3. Does not pull out right away.
4. Does not withdraw while the penis is still erect.
5. Does not leave space at the end of condom (so it will not break).

Advantages
Effective, safe, can be purchased at a drugstore; excellent protection against sexually transmitted infections.

Disadvantages
- Objectionable to some men and women.
- Interrupts intercourse.
- May be messy.
- Condom may break.
- Rarely, individuals are allergic to rubber. If this is a problem, condoms called "skins" which are not made out of rubber are available.

Effectiveness rate:
Proper use:
90% effective
About 85% effective if used correctly and consistently, but much less effective if used carelessly.

Poor use:
64%

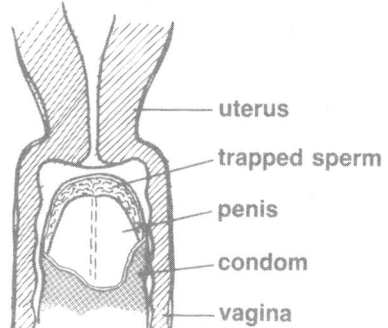

- uterus
- trapped sperm
- penis
- condom
- vagina

FOAM, JELLIES, CREAMS

What it is
SPERMICIDAL FOAM, JELLY OR CREAM
Cream and jelly come in tubes; foam comes in aerosol cans or individual applicators and is placed in to the vagina.

How it works
Foam, jelly and cream contain a chemical that kills sperm and acts as a physical barrier between sperm and the uterus.

How to use it
Put foam, jelly or cream into your vagina each time you have intercourse, not more than 30 minutes beforehand. No douching for at least 8 hours after intercourse.

You will get pregnant if you:
- don't insert immediately before sex
- douche immediately after intercourse
- don't follow directions

Advantages
Effective, safe, a good lubricant and can be purchased at a drugstore.

Disadvantages
Must be inserted just before intercourse. Some find it inconvenient or messy.

Some women find that the foam, cream or jelly irritates the vagina. May irritate the man's penis. Try changing brands if this happens.

Effectiveness rate:
Proper use:
About 80-90% effective if used correctly and consistently, but much less effective if used carelessly.

Poor use:
60%

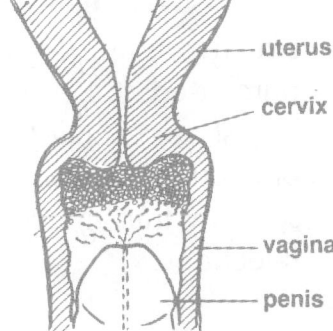

CONDOM & FOAM TOGETHER

What it is
CONDOM AND FOAM USED TOGETHER

How it works
Prevents sperm from getting inside the uterus by killing sperm and by preventing sperm from getting out into the vagina.

How to use it
Foam must be inserted within 30 minutes before intercourse and condom must be placed onto erect penis prior to contact with the vagina.

You will get pregnant if you:
- don't use the condom correctly
- don't use foam correctly

Advantages
Extremely effective, safe, and both methods may be purchased at a drugstore without a doctor's prescription. Excellent protection against sexually transmitted infections.

Disadvantages
Requires more effort than some couples like. May be messy or inconvenient. Interrupts intercourse.

No serious complications.

Effectiveness rate:
Proper use

Close to 100% effective if both foam and condoms are used with every act of intercourse.

Poor use:

80%

THE IUD

What it is
INTRAUTERINE DEVICE (IUD)
A small piece of plastic with nylon threads attached. Some have copper wire wrapped around them. One IUD gives off a hormone, progesterone.

How it works
The IUD is inserted into the uterus. It is not known exactly how the IUD prevents pregnancy.

How to use it
You must check string at least once a month right after the period ends to make sure your IUD is still properly in place.

You will get pregnant if:
The IUD comes out and you haven't checked the string and think you are protected.

Advantages
- Effective
- Always there when needed
- Usually not felt by either partner

Disadvantages
Must be inserted by a doctor after a pelvic examination. Cannot be used by all women. Sometimes the uterus "pushes" it out.
- May cause cramps, bleeding, or spotting.
- Infections of the uterus or of the oviducts (tubes) may be serious.
* See a doctor for pain, bleeding, fever, or a bad discharge.

Effectiveness rate:
Proper use:
97-99% if patient checks for string regularly.

Poor use:
1-3% (if IUD is expelled)

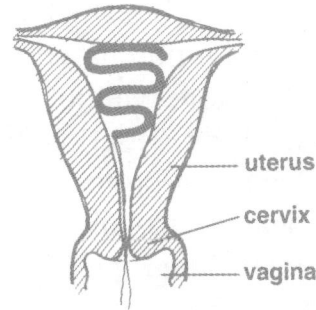

- uterus
- cervix
- vagina

INDEX

Abdominal pains, 83
Abortion, 8, 144
Abstinence, 174, 180
Advice, 103
Afterbirth, 23,32
Alcohol, 81,82
All day sickness, 43
Amniotic fluid, 32
Amniotic sac, 32
Anemia, 61
Anger, 89
Aspirin, 82
Baby sick, 162
Back strain, 67
Backache, 39,53
Bacteria, 45
Bag of waters, 23, 32
Basic four food groups, 63
Birth, 134
Birth canal, 78
Birth classes, 122
Birthmarks, 81
Bladder, 37,46
Blood, 75
Blood pressure, 77
Body image, 92
Boyfriend, 102
Breastfeeding, 37,79,158,159
Breasts, 79
Breathing, 55,126,128, 129,130
Burping, 159
Calcium 40,54
Cat's litter box, 83
Cell, 30

Cervix, 26,28,45,77,123
Cesarean, C-section, 3,9,133
Childbirth, 119
Childbirth classes, 8,21
Chills, 83
Choices in parenting, 143
Chromosome, 28
Climax, 27
Coach, 130,131
Colostrum, 37
Community, 101,103
Conception, 25,27
Condom, 28,174,180, 183,185
Condom and foam, 180
Constipation, 35,38,48
Contraceptives, 4,21,165, 172-174,176-178
Contracting, contractions 44,123,124,134
Cramps, 35,54
Creams, 183
Cycle, 26
Dating, 95
Delivery room, 138
Diaphragm, 28,174,179,182
Diarrhea, 124
Diet, 80
Digestive system, 33
Dilatation, 124
Discharge, 44,124
Disease, 83
Doctor, 160
Dominant genes, 28
Douche, 45

Drinking, 46
Drugs, 81,82,87
Due date, 35,40
Eating right, 58,59
Education, 107
Effacement, 124
Egg, 23, 25-28
Ejaculation, 27
Embryo, 25,33
Emotional, 88
Empty calories, 65
Erect, erection, 27
Exercise, 51,57,66,68,126
Expulsion, 125,132
Fallopian tube, 25-27,30
Family, 99,102
Fast food, 63
Fatigue, 47
Fear, 90
Fertilization, 27
Fertilize, 25
Fetal Organs, 33
Fetal development, 33
Fetal exam, 80
Fetus, 33
Fever, 83
Fluid from vagina, 83
Foam, 175,183,185
Food, 60
Fraternal twins, 29
Friends, 93,100,102
G.E.D. diploma, 115
Gas, 38
Genes, 28
Genitals, 27

Gums, teeth, 79, 82
Headache, 82
Heart, 78
Heartburn, 38,49
Hemoglobin, 61
Hemorrhoids, 38
Hormones, 37,39,44
Hospital, 132
Husband, 102
IUD, 174,180,186
Identical twins, 29
Implanting, 43
Indigestion, 44
Infection, 61
Intercourse, 25,27,173
Jellies, 183
Jobs, 114
Junk food, 57,65
Kidney infection, 46
Labor, 40,122
Lamaze classes, 92,122
Ligaments, 38, 52
Lightening, 55
Lines from boys, 168,169
Lines to say, "No", 170
Marijuana, 82
Marriage, 143,149
Married parenting, 144
Mask of pregnancy, 38
Measurements, 33
Medication, 82
Menstruate, menstruation, 23,26
Miscarriage, 73
Morning sickness, 35,37,43

Mucous, 45,124
Muscle cramps, 40
Myths, 81
Nausea, 37,43
Navel, 32
Newborn, 153
Nipples, 79
Nutrition, 20,57,81
Obstetric exam, 77,78,80
Odor, 45
Orgasm, 27
Ovary, ovaries, 25,26
Ovulation, 25-27, 40
Pains, 52,122
Parenting alternatives, 143
Parents, 96
Partner, 99,102
Pelvic floor, 38,70
Pelvic joints, 39
Pelvic tilt, 68
Pelvis, 78
Penis, 27
Period, 26,37
Phases of labor, 124
Pill, 174,178,181

Placenta, 30,32,33,37, 59,125
Position, 126,132,133
Postpartum, 125
Posture, 53,66,67
Prenatal care, 20,73
Prenatal clinic, 100
Prenatal exam, 3,73,75
Professionals, 103
Protein, 64
Pubic bone, 25,77
Recessive, 28
Relaxation, 71,125-127,132
Relinquishment, 143, 147,150
Rest, 71
Rh positive or negative, 75
Rhythm birth control, 175,180
Sacrum, 77
School, 101,102,107, 109,115
Semen, 27
Sex, 167
Sexuality, 21

Shortness of breath, 70
Single parenting, 143,146,149
Sleep, 71
Smoking, 81
Social changes, 92
Socially transmitted disease, 177
Spasms, 54
Sperm, 23,25,27,28
Spermacidal jelly, 28
Spray cans, 83
Sterile, sterility, 5
Stillbirth, 73
Stress, 85,87
Stretch marks, 35,40,50
Support, 97,102
Suppositories, 180
Swelling, 37,69,83
Teen parenting program, 110
Teeth, 79
Tenderness, 37
Testes, Testicles, 27
Toxemia, 47,73,91
Transition, 124,137

Travel, 82
Trimesters, 88
Twins, 29
Umbilical cord, 30,32,33, 37,81
Urethra, 27
Urinate, 37,46,132
Uterus, 23,25,26,28,30 37,44,72,78,123
VD, 177
Vagina, 26,44,77,78
Vaginal bleeding, 83
Varicose veins, 35,38,51
Venereal disease, VD, 83
Vision, dim or blurred, 83
Visualization, 126,127
Vocational training, 107, 114,115
Vomiting, 44,83
Vulva, 77
Water retention, 49
Weight gain, baby's, 39
Welfare, 109
What can go wrong?, 133
X-rays, 82
Zits, 62